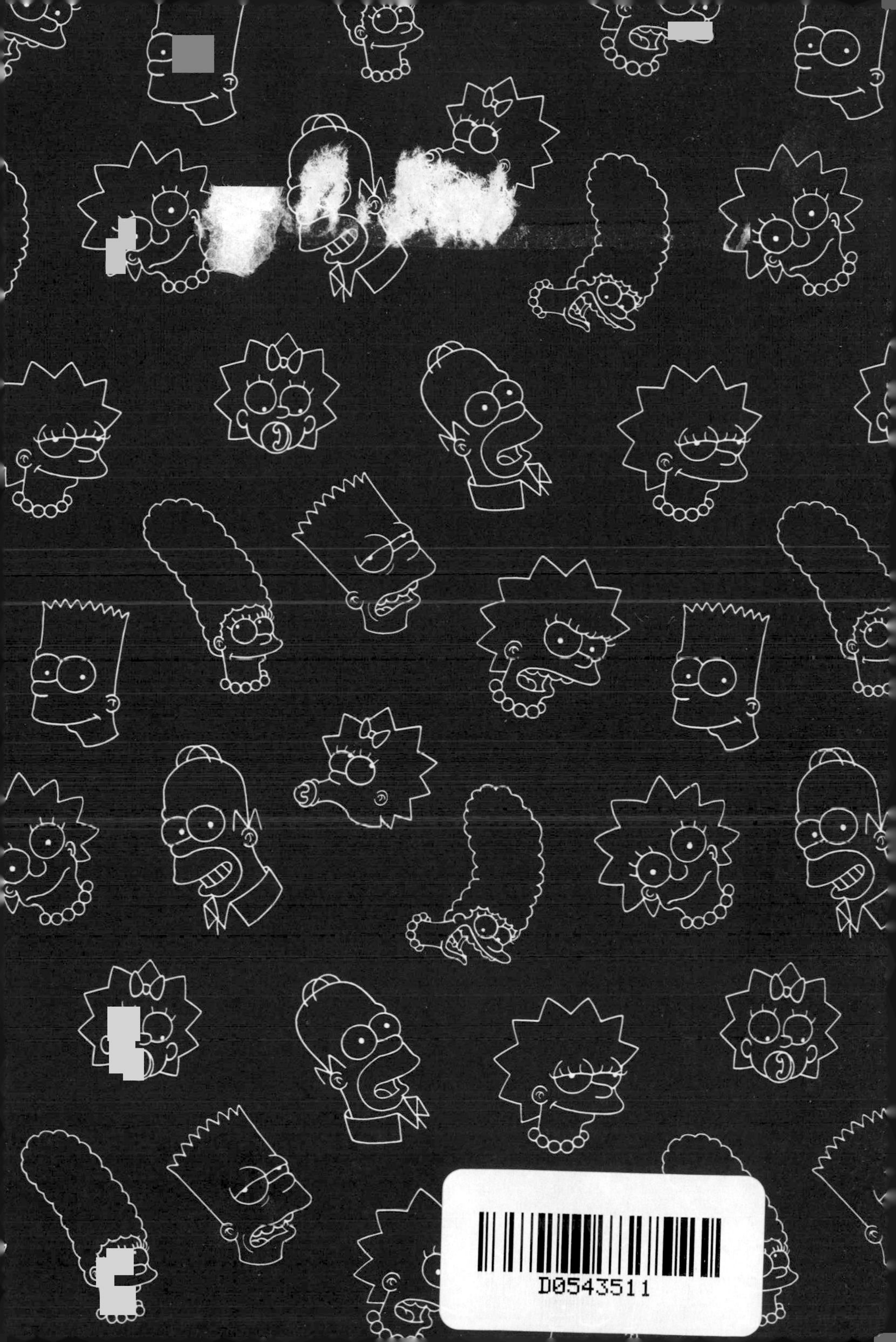

SIMPSONS™
COMICS EXTRAVAGANZA

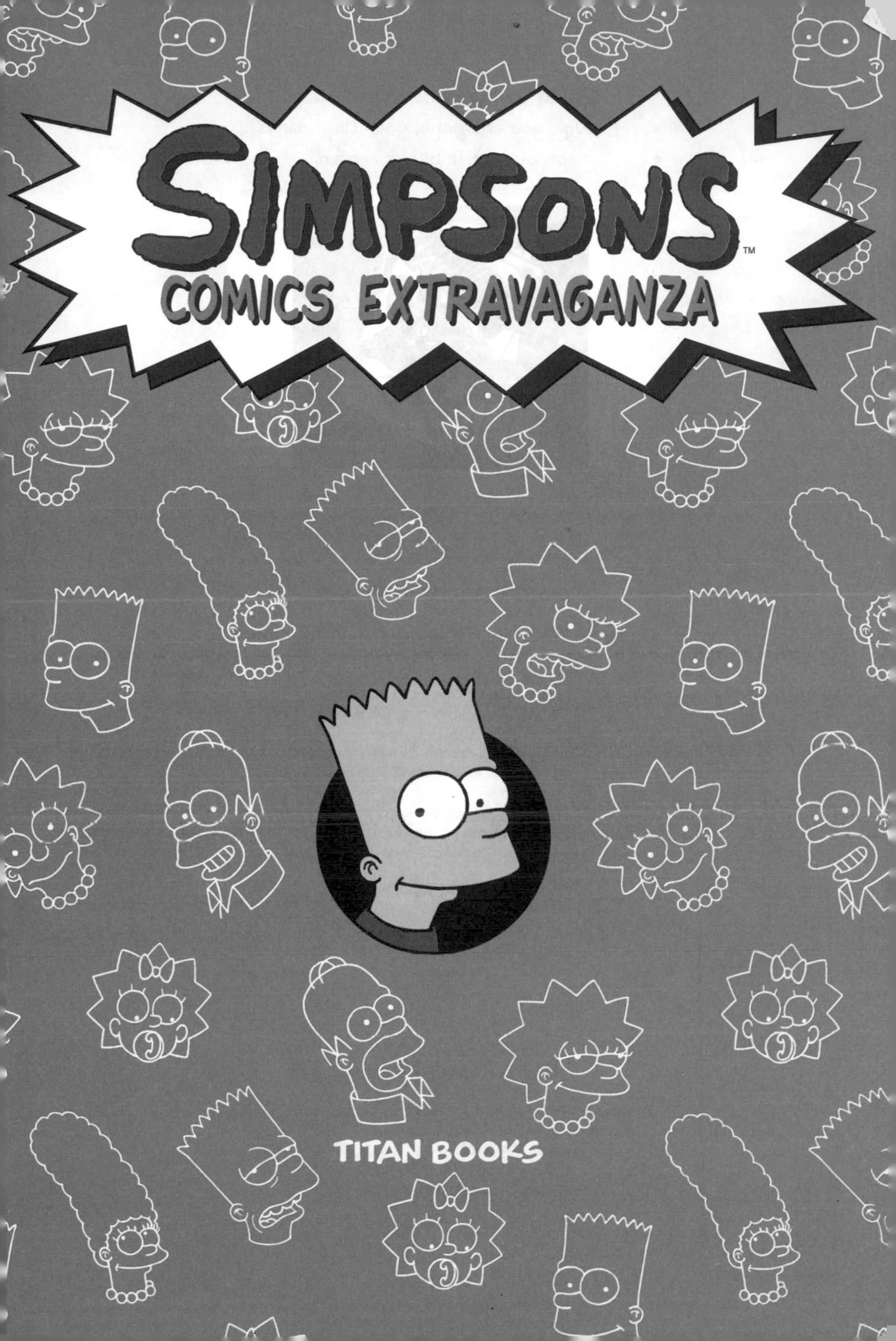

TITAN BOOKS

Dedicated to the memory of Snowball I:
Though you are gone, your claw marks
on our comic books remain.

SIMPSONS COMICS EXTRAVAGANZA

Bongo Comics Group c/o Titan Books
P.O. Box 1963, Santa Monica, CA 90406-1963

Published in the UK by Titan Books, a division of Titan Publishing Group, 144 Southwark St., London, SE1 0UP, under licence from Bongo Entertainment, Inc.

FIRST EDITION: MARCH 2008

ISBN-10: 1 84576 718 7
ISBN-13: 9781845767181

2 4 6 8 10 9 7 5 3 1

Publisher: MATT GROENING
Editors in Chief/Creative Directors: STEVE VANCE, CINDY VANCE
Managing Editor: JASON GRODE
Art Director: BILL MORRISON
Contributing Artists: TIM BAVINGTON, PHIL ORTIZ, SONDRA ROY
Contributing Writers: DEB LUCUSTA, DAN CASTELLANETA
Book Design: MARILYN FRANDSEN, DEBORAH ROSS
Publicity Director: ANTONIA COFFMAN
Legal Guardian: SUSAN A. GRODE

Printed in Spain

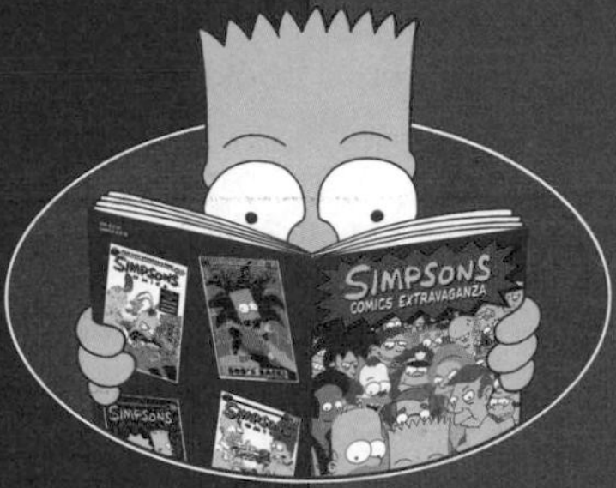
SIMPSONS
COMICS EXTRAVAGANZA

CONTENTS

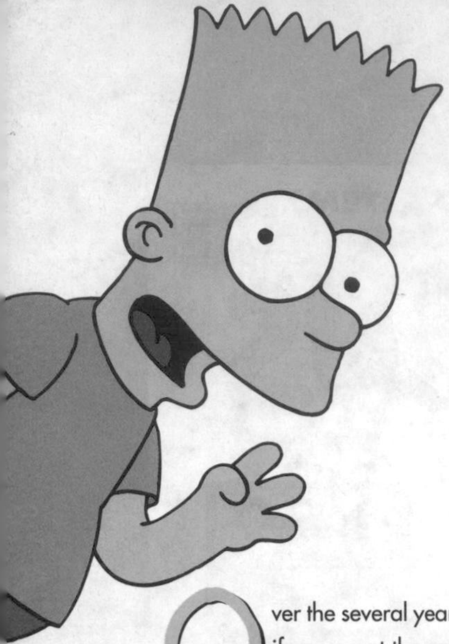

WELCOME TO SIMPSONS COMICS EXTRAVAGANZA, MAN!

Over the several years that the Simpsons have been cavorting on TV (since 1987, if you count the prehistoric shorts on the "Tracey Ullman Show"), we've gotten the kinds of compliments that cartoonists crave hearing: you're setting a bad example, you're corrupting youth, you're frightening Americans about nuclear power, you're hastening the downfall of western civilization. But my favorite prissy outrage at Simpsonian subversion came in 1990, when school principals, busybodies, and petty government officials across the land flipped out because of the Bart Simpson underachiever T-shirts—you know the ones, with Bart saying "And proud of it, man!"

The point of that T-shirt was that no kids call themselves underachievers—that's a label middle-achieving grown-ups slap on mischief-achieving kids. And the proper wisenheimer response to being labeled an underachiever, of course, is to be "proud of it, man!" Of course, none of the Simpsons critics gave us any credit when we followed up the Bart Simpson Underachiever T-shirt with a Lisa Simpson Overachiever T-shirt. But that may be because on that T-shirt we had Lisa saying, "Damn I'm good!"

Which brings me to the Simpsons Comics Extravaganza. This consists of the remarkable first four issues of Simpsons Comics, brought to you by the Bongo Comics Group, a small but overachieving band of merry artists, designers, lawyers, and publicists, namely: Steve Vance, Cindy Vance, Bill Morrison, Jason Grode, Susan Grode, and Antonia Coffman. Their work looks effortless, but believe me, the Bongo gang has shed several droplets of sweat, a few driplets of blood, and perhaps even a couple tears of joy in the making of these comics. Don't worry, however: All Bongo bodily secretions have been wiped off the original art so as not to distract you from your entertainment experience.

As Bart might say, We're proud of these comics, man. As Lisa might say, Damn, they're good.

And as Marge might say, I don't want you sitting up in that treehouse all day reading comic books! You'll ruin your eyes!

MATT GROENING

Bongo Comics Group

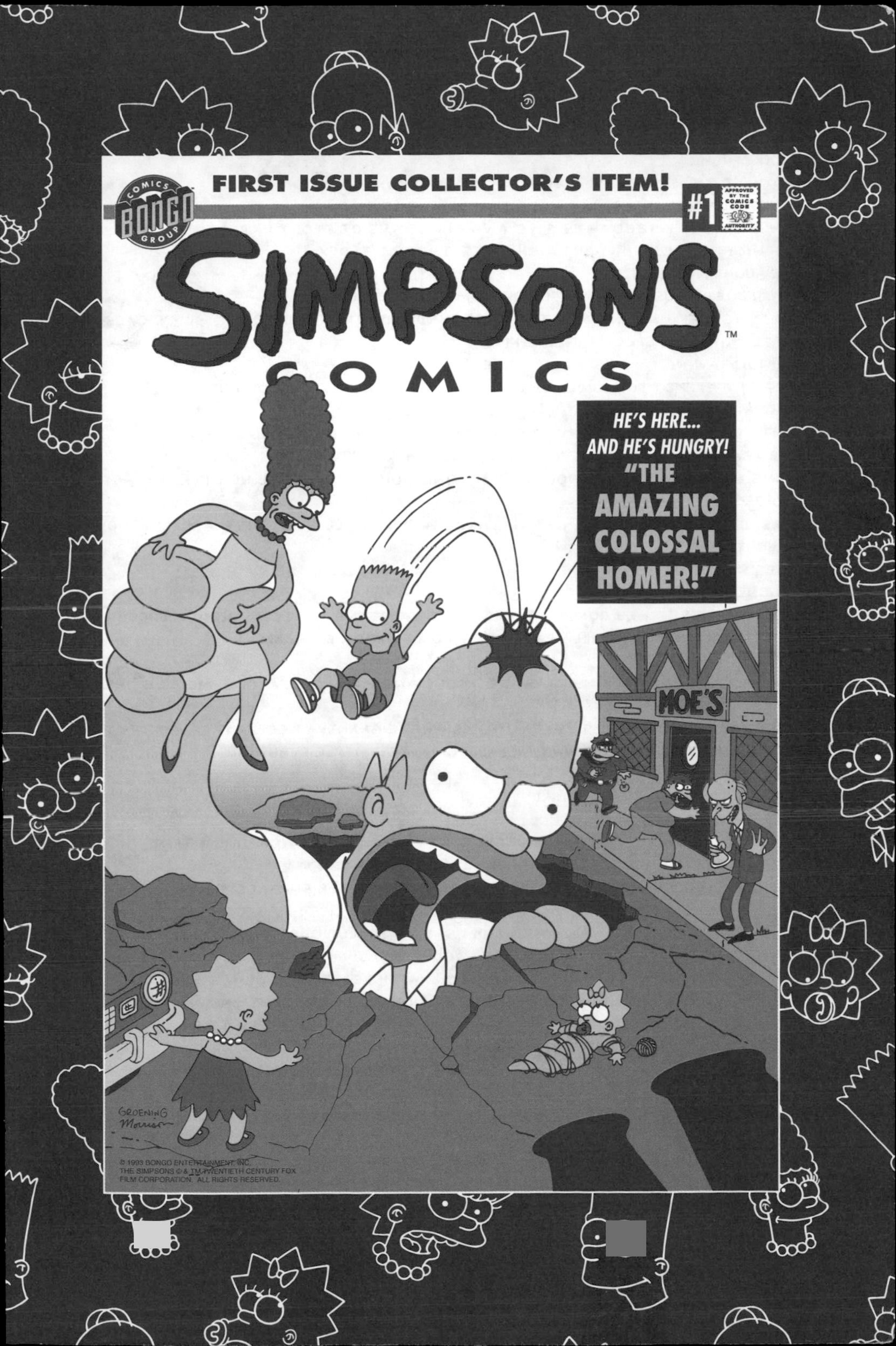

FIRST ISSUE COLLECTOR'S ITEM!
COMICS BONGO GROUP
#1
APPROVED BY THE COMICS CODE AUTHORITY
SIMPSONS™
COMICS
HE'S HERE... AND HE'S HUNGRY!
"THE AMAZING COLOSSAL HOMER!"
MOE'S
GROENING
Morrison
© 1993 BONGO ENTERTAINMENT, INC.
THE SIMPSONS © & TM TWENTIETH CENTURY FOX
FILM CORPORATION. ALL RIGHTS RESERVED.

BART'S BOTTOM 40

1. LISA'S SAXOPHONE
2. VEGETABLES THAT DON'T FLY WELL OFF YOUR SPOON
3. WRINKLED OLD GROWNUPS - - I HOPE I NEVER BECOME ONE
4. THE CHEAP LOUSY PRIZES THEY GIVE AWAY IN BOXES OF FROSTY KRUSTY FLAKES
5. HAVING NIGHTMARES THAT I'M A CHIP OFF THE OLD BLOCK
6. BEING CAUGHT RED-HANDED
7. THE HARDENED CRUST ON THE TOP OF MOM'S CASSEROLES
8. THE GOOEY STUFF UNDERNEATH THE HARDENED CRUST ON THE TOP OF MOM'S CASSEROLES
9. PRINCIPAL SKINNER'S SPECIAL FILE ON ME
10. THE "NO DRAWING ON THE WALL" RULE
11. THE FACT THAT OTTO HARDLY EVER LETS ME DRIVE THE SCHOOL BUS
12. CREAMED CORN
13. PARENTS WHO HAVE SIGNATURES THAT ARE REALLY HARD TO FORGE
14. ACCIDENTALLY FEELING GUM STUCK UNDERNEATH A RESTAURANT TABLE
15. SUCKING ON YOUR PEN IN SCHOOL AND HAVING YOUR MOUTH FILL UP WITH INK
16. NAMBY-PAMBY G-RATED MOVIES
17. DAD'S SNORING THAT YOU CAN HEAR THROUGH THE WALL EVEN WITH A PILLOW COVERING YOUR HEAD
18. STORIES WITH MORALS AT THE END
19. CARTOONS WITH NO FUN VIOLENCE AND PAIN
20. CARTOONS WHERE THEY RUN PAST THE SAME LAMP AND TABLE A ZILLION TIMES
21. THE STRAWBERRY AND VANILLA PARTS OF NEOPOLITAN ICE CREAM
22. GAS STATION RESTROOMS
23. MAKING BAD WORDS WITH MY ALPHABET SOUP AND HAVING LISA TELL ME THEY'RE MISSPELLED
24. ACCIDENTALLY DRINKING OUT OF THE GLASS WHERE GRANDPA KEEPS HIS FALSE TEETH
25. THE DIFFICULTY OF LOADING WATER BALLOONS WITH MAPLE SYRUP
26. SUGARLESS ANYTHING
27. BEING TRIED IN COURT AS AN ADULT
28. VENGEFUL BARBERS
29. THE HAUNTING THOUGHT THAT SIDESHOW BOB WILL GET OUT OF JAIL AGAIN
30. RIP-OFF CHOCOLATE BUNNIES THAT ARE HOLLOW INSIDE
31. COMIC BOOKS WITH INSUFFICIENTLY GIMMICKY COVER ENHANCEMENTS
32. PHLEGM (ALSO ON MY TOP 40 LIST)
33. WHEN MOM SAYS "IF ALL YOUR FRIENDS JUMPED OFF THE BRIDGE, WOULD YOU JUMP TOO?"
34. CARTOONS WITH REDEEMING SOCIAL MESSAGES
35. THE NONEDIBLE DECORATIONS ON BIRTHDAY CAKES THAT YOU ACCIDENTALLY TRY TO EAT
36. BRUSSELS SPROUTS
37. FORGETTING ABOUT THE CANDY BAR YOU PUT IN YOUR PANTS POCKET ON A REALLY HOT DAY
38. SWIMMING POOL BELLY-FLOPS THAT BOTH HURT AND LOOK DUMB
39. THE BOTTOMS OF YOUR SNEAKERS AFTER YOU COME OUT OF A PETTING ZOO
40. BEING AN "UNDERACHIEVER" - - TO TELL YOU THE TRUTH, I'M NOT EXACTLY SURE WHAT THE WORD MEANS

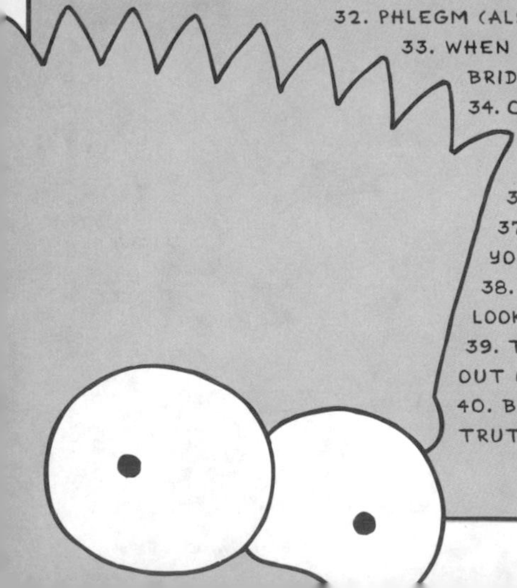

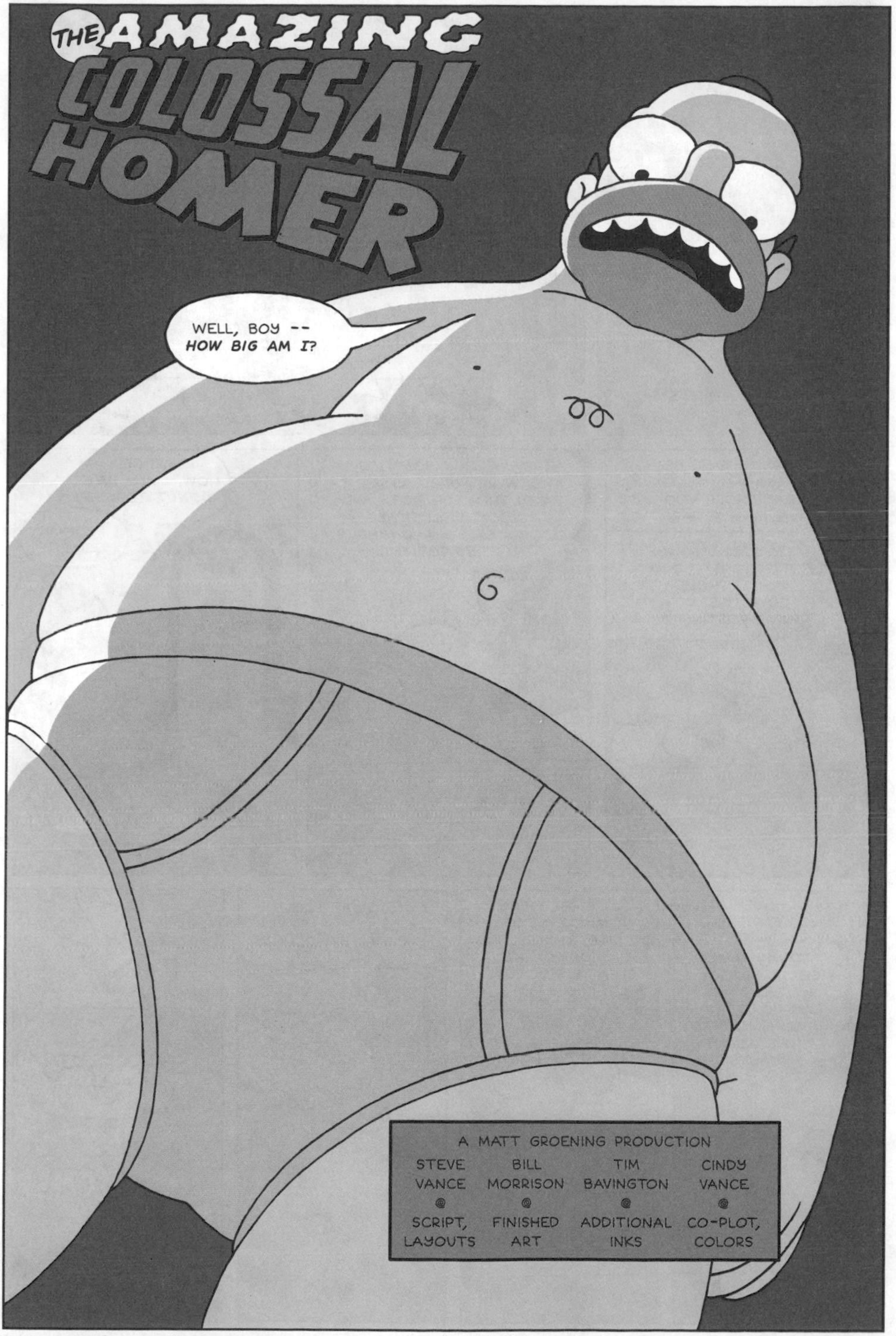
THE AMAZING COLOSSAL HOMER
WELL, BOY -- HOW BIG AM I?
A MATT GROENING PRODUCTION
STEVE VANCE @ SCRIPT, LAYOUTS
BILL MORRISON @ FINISHED ART
TIM BAVINGTON @ ADDITIONAL INKS
CINDY VANCE @ CO-PLOT, COLORS

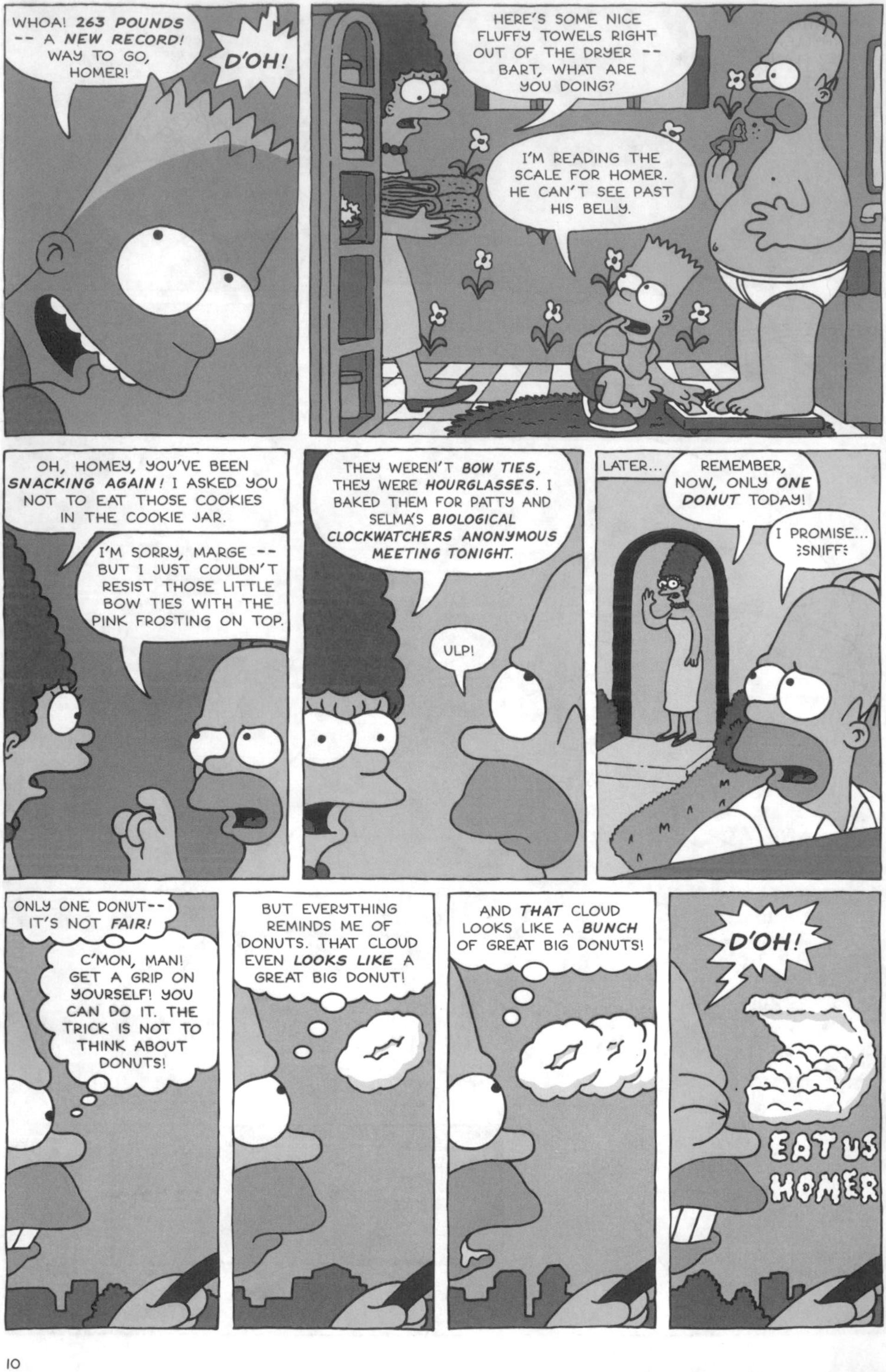
WHOA! 263 POUNDS -- A NEW RECORD! WAY TO GO, HOMER!
D'OH!
HERE'S SOME NICE FLUFFY TOWELS RIGHT OUT OF THE DRYER -- BART, WHAT ARE YOU DOING?
I'M READING THE SCALE FOR HOMER. HE CAN'T SEE PAST HIS BELLY.
OH, HOMEY, YOU'VE BEEN SNACKING AGAIN! I ASKED YOU NOT TO EAT THOSE COOKIES IN THE COOKIE JAR.
I'M SORRY, MARGE -- BUT I JUST COULDN'T RESIST THOSE LITTLE BOW TIES WITH THE PINK FROSTING ON TOP.
THEY WEREN'T BOW TIES, THEY WERE HOURGLASSES. I BAKED THEM FOR PATTY AND SELMA'S BIOLOGICAL CLOCKWATCHERS ANONYMOUS MEETING TONIGHT.
ULP!
LATER...
REMEMBER, NOW, ONLY ONE DONUT TODAY!
I PROMISE... SNIFF
ONLY ONE DONUT-- IT'S NOT FAIR!
C'MON, MAN! GET A GRIP ON YOURSELF! YOU CAN DO IT. THE TRICK IS NOT TO THINK ABOUT DONUTS!
BUT EVERYTHING REMINDS ME OF DONUTS. THAT CLOUD EVEN LOOKS LIKE A GREAT BIG DONUT!
AND THAT CLOUD LOOKS LIKE A BUNCH OF GREAT BIG DONUTS!
D'OH!
EAT US HOMER

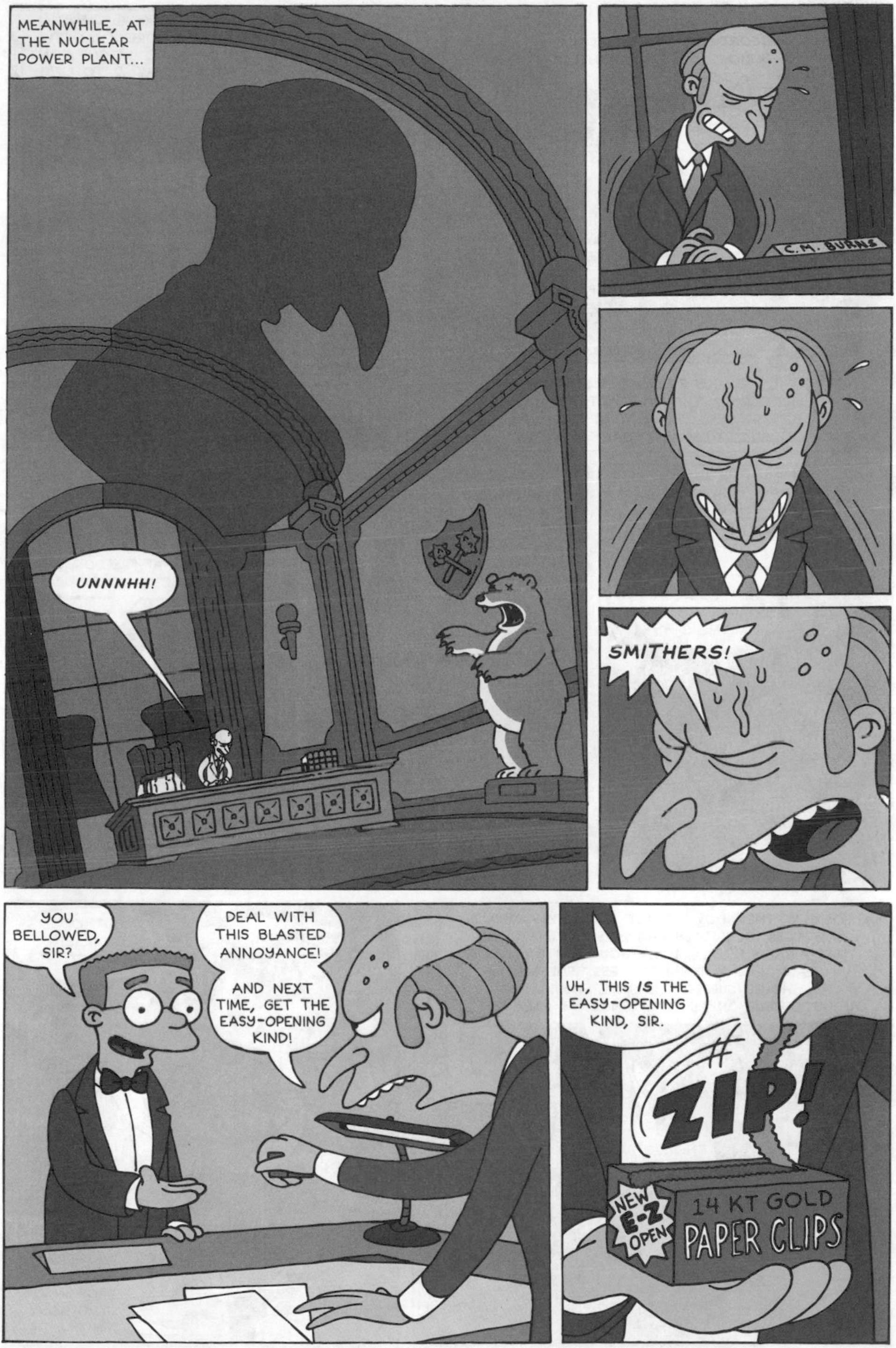
MEANWHILE, AT THE NUCLEAR POWER PLANT...
UNNNHH!
C.M. BURNS
SMITHERS!
YOU BELLOWED, SIR?
DEAL WITH THIS BLASTED ANNOYANCE!
AND NEXT TIME, GET THE EASY-OPENING KIND!
UH, THIS *IS* THE EASY-OPENING KIND, SIR.
ZIP!
NEW E-Z OPEN
14 KT GOLD PAPER CLIPS

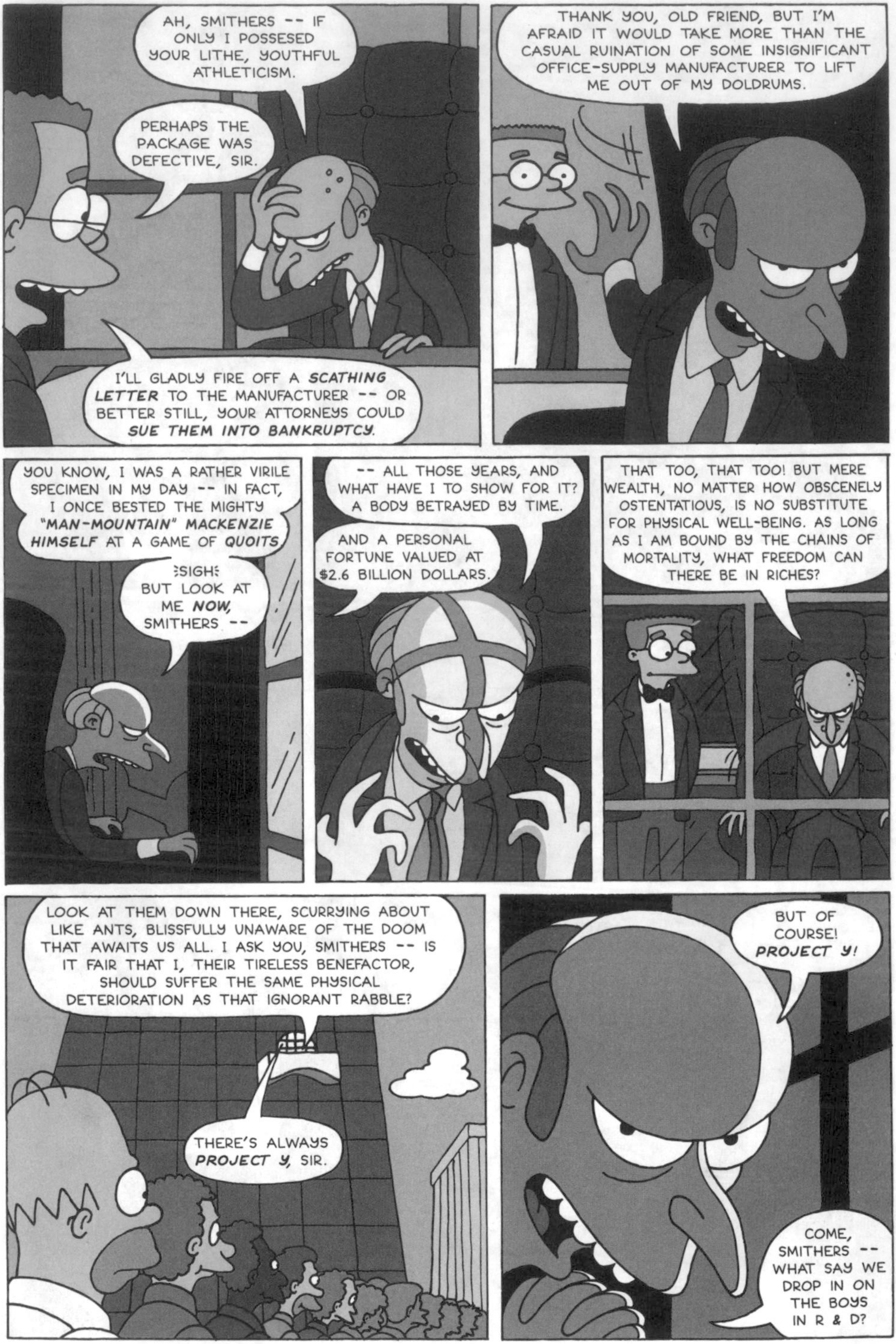

AH, SMITHERS -- IF ONLY I POSSESED YOUR LITHE, YOUTHFUL ATHLETICISM.
PERHAPS THE PACKAGE WAS DEFECTIVE, SIR.
I'LL GLADLY FIRE OFF A **SCATHING LETTER** TO THE MANUFACTURER -- OR BETTER STILL, YOUR ATTORNEYS COULD **SUE THEM INTO BANKRUPTCY**.
THANK YOU, OLD FRIEND, BUT I'M AFRAID IT WOULD TAKE MORE THAN THE CASUAL RUINATION OF SOME INSIGNIFICANT OFFICE-SUPPLY MANUFACTURER TO LIFT ME OUT OF MY DOLDRUMS.
YOU KNOW, I WAS A RATHER VIRILE SPECIMEN IN MY DAY -- IN FACT, I ONCE BESTED THE MIGHTY **"MAN-MOUNTAIN" MACKENZIE HIMSELF** AT A GAME OF **QUOITS**.
:SIGH: BUT LOOK AT ME **NOW**, SMITHERS --
-- ALL THOSE YEARS, AND WHAT HAVE I TO SHOW FOR IT? A BODY BETRAYED BY TIME.
AND A PERSONAL FORTUNE VALUED AT $2.6 BILLION DOLLARS.
THAT TOO, THAT TOO! BUT MERE WEALTH, NO MATTER HOW OBSCENELY OSTENTATIOUS, IS NO SUBSTITUTE FOR PHYSICAL WELL-BEING. AS LONG AS I AM BOUND BY THE CHAINS OF MORTALITY, WHAT FREEDOM CAN THERE BE IN RICHES?
LOOK AT THEM DOWN THERE, SCURRYING ABOUT LIKE ANTS, BLISSFULLY UNAWARE OF THE DOOM THAT AWAITS US ALL. I ASK YOU, SMITHERS -- IS IT FAIR THAT I, THEIR TIRELESS BENEFACTOR, SHOULD SUFFER THE SAME PHYSICAL DETERIORATION AS THAT IGNORANT RABBLE?
THERE'S ALWAYS **PROJECT Y**, SIR.
BUT OF COURSE! **PROJECT Y!**
COME, SMITHERS -- WHAT SAY WE DROP IN ON THE BOYS IN R & D?

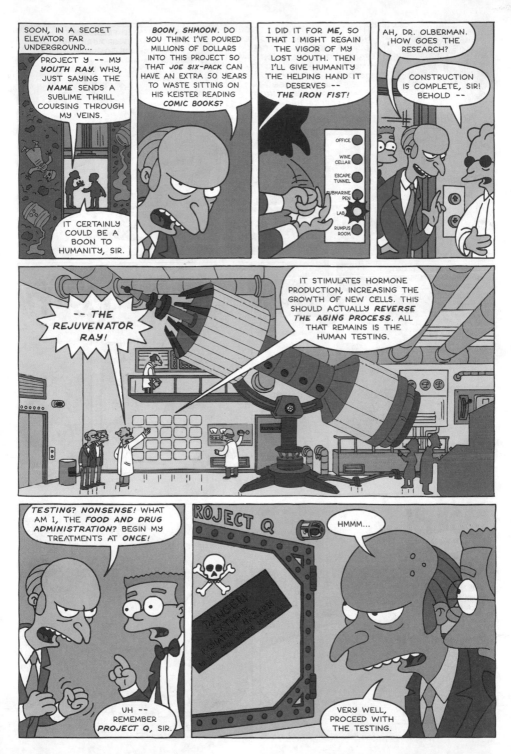

SOON, IN A SECRET ELEVATOR FAR UNDERGROUND...

PROJECT Y -- MY *YOUTH RAY*. WHY, JUST SAYING THE *NAME* SENDS A SUBLIME THRILL COURSING THROUGH MY VEINS.

IT CERTAINLY COULD BE A BOON TO HUMANITY, SIR.

BOON, SHMOON. DO YOU THINK I'VE POURED MILLIONS OF DOLLARS INTO THIS PROJECT SO THAT *JOE SIX-PACK* CAN HAVE AN EXTRA 50 YEARS TO WASTE SITTING ON HIS KEISTER READING *COMIC BOOKS*?

I DID IT FOR *ME*, SO THAT I MIGHT REGAIN THE VIGOR OF MY LOST YOUTH. THEN I'LL GIVE HUMANITY THE HELPING HAND IT DESERVES -- *THE IRON FIST!*

OFFICE
WINE CELLAR
ESCAPE TUNNEL
SUBMARINE PEN
LAB
RUMPUS ROOM

AH, DR. OLBERMAN. HOW GOES THE RESEARCH?

CONSTRUCTION IS COMPLETE, SIR! BEHOLD --

-- THE REJUVENATOR RAY!

IT STIMULATES HORMONE PRODUCTION, INCREASING THE GROWTH OF NEW CELLS. THIS SHOULD ACTUALLY *REVERSE THE AGING PROCESS*. ALL THAT REMAINS IS THE HUMAN TESTING.

TESTING? *NONSENSE!* WHAT AM I, THE *FOOD AND DRUG ADMINISTRATION*? BEGIN MY TREATMENTS AT *ONCE!*

UH -- REMEMBER *PROJECT Q*, SIR.

PROJECT Q

DANGER! EXTREME RADIATION HAZARD!

HMMM...

VERY WELL, PROCEED WITH THE TESTING.

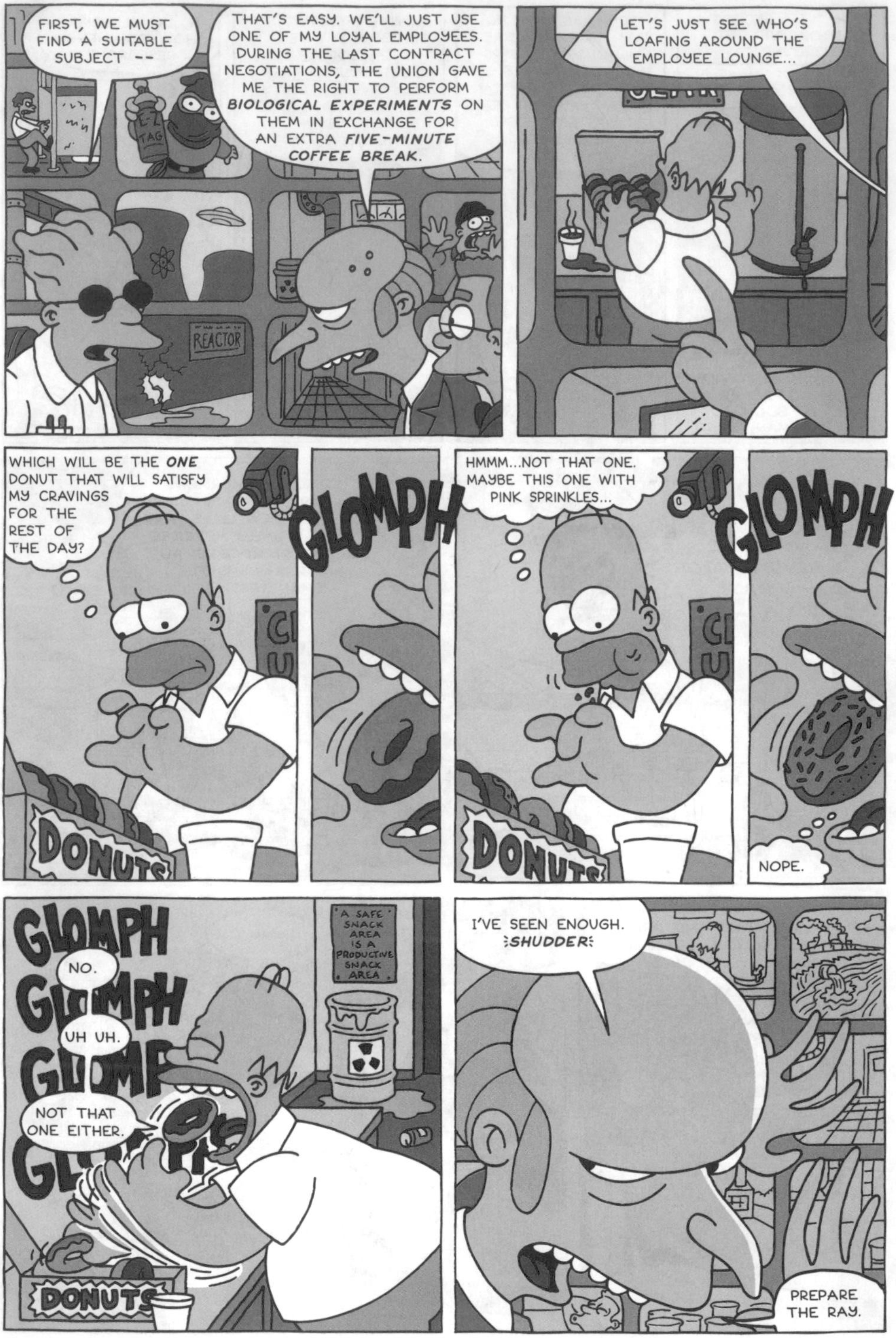
FIRST, WE MUST FIND A SUITABLE SUBJECT --
THAT'S EASY. WE'LL JUST USE ONE OF MY LOYAL EMPLOYEES. DURING THE LAST CONTRACT NEGOTIATIONS, THE UNION GAVE ME THE RIGHT TO PERFORM BIOLOGICAL EXPERIMENTS ON THEM IN EXCHANGE FOR AN EXTRA FIVE-MINUTE COFFEE BREAK.
REACTOR
LET'S JUST SEE WHO'S LOAFING AROUND THE EMPLOYEE LOUNGE...
WHICH WILL BE THE ONE DONUT THAT WILL SATISFY MY CRAVINGS FOR THE REST OF THE DAY?
DONUTS
GLOMPH
HMMM...NOT THAT ONE. MAYBE THIS ONE WITH PINK SPRINKLES...
DONUTS
GLOMPH
NOPE.
GLOMPH
NO.
GLOMPH
UH UH.
GLOMP
NOT THAT ONE EITHER.
A SAFE SNACK AREA IS A PRODUCTIVE SNACK AREA
DONUTS
I'VE SEEN ENOUGH. SHUDDER
PREPARE THE RAY.

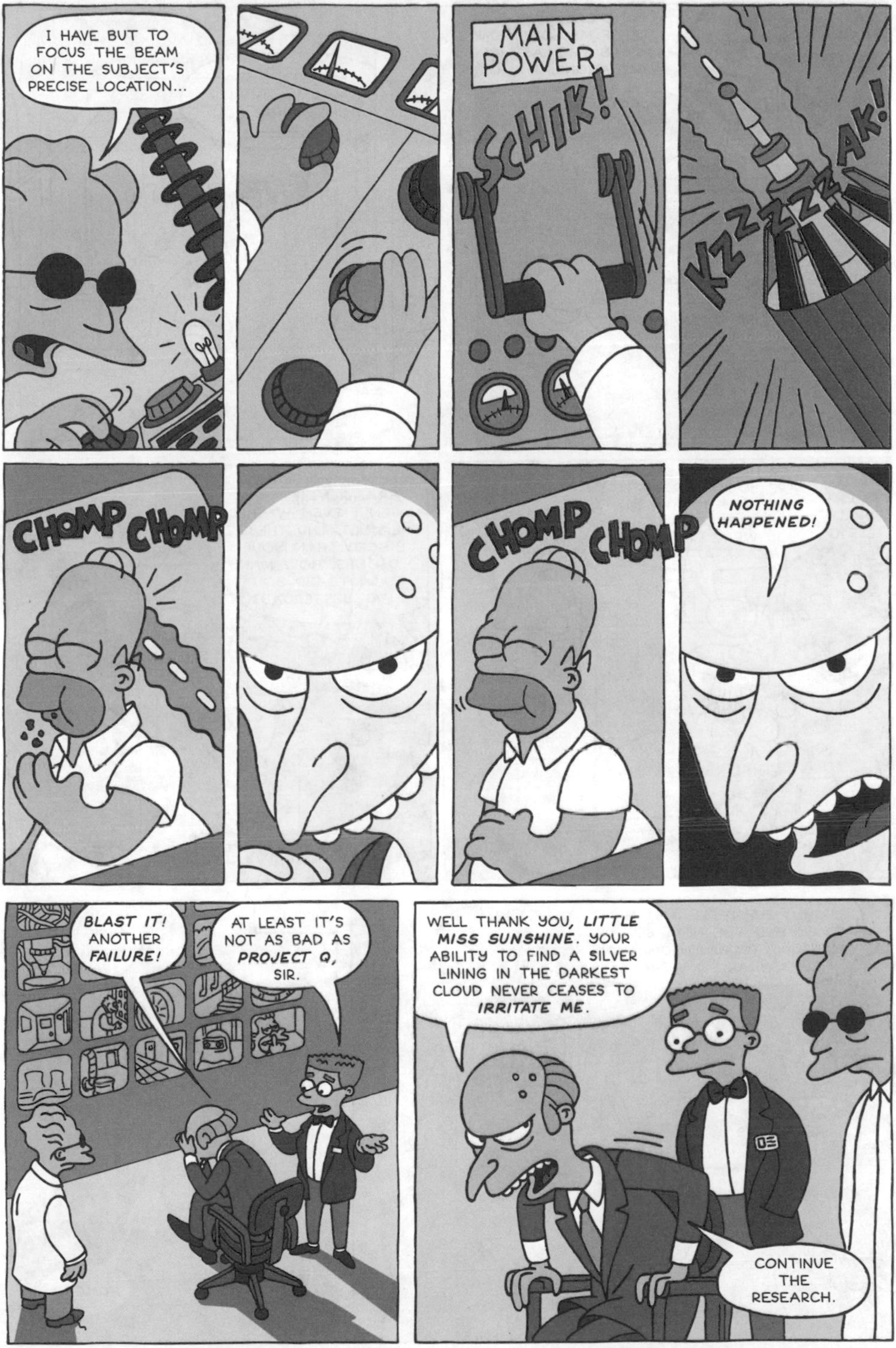
I HAVE BUT TO FOCUS THE BEAM ON THE SUBJECT'S PRECISE LOCATION...
MAIN POWER
SCHIK!
KZZZZZZAK!
CHOMP CHOMP
CHOMP CHOMP
NOTHING HAPPENED!
BLAST IT! ANOTHER FAILURE!
AT LEAST IT'S NOT AS BAD AS PROJECT Q, SIR.
WELL THANK YOU, LITTLE MISS SUNSHINE. YOUR ABILITY TO FIND A SILVER LINING IN THE DARKEST CLOUD NEVER CEASES TO IRRITATE ME.
CONTINUE THE RESEARCH.

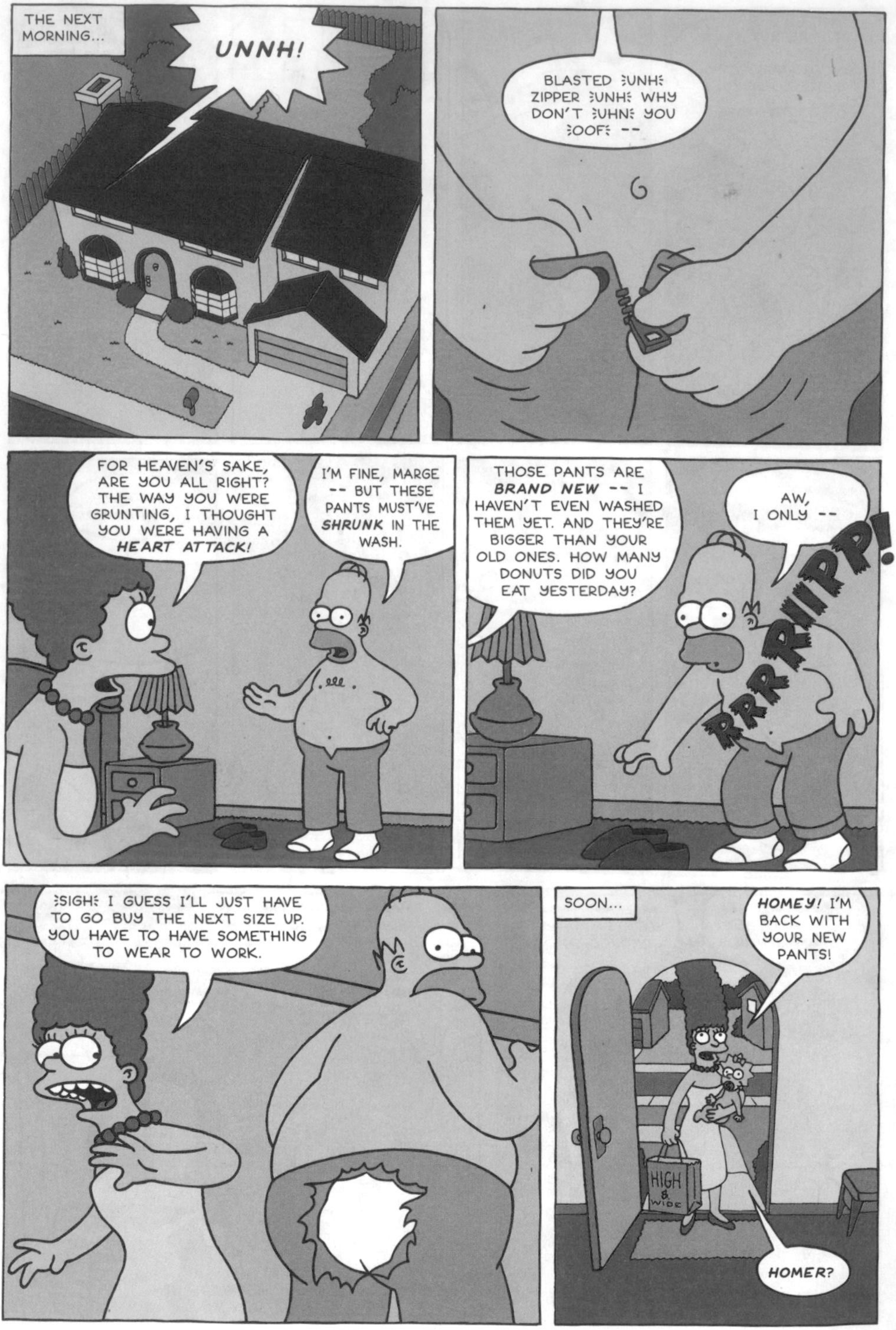
THE NEXT MORNING...
UNNH!
BLASTED ⁝UNH⁝ ZIPPER ⁝UNH⁝ WHY DON'T ⁝UHN⁝ YOU ⁝OOF⁝ --
FOR HEAVEN'S SAKE, ARE YOU ALL RIGHT? THE WAY YOU WERE GRUNTING, I THOUGHT YOU WERE HAVING A HEART ATTACK!
I'M FINE, MARGE -- BUT THESE PANTS MUST'VE SHRUNK IN THE WASH.
THOSE PANTS ARE BRAND NEW -- I HAVEN'T EVEN WASHED THEM YET. AND THEY'RE BIGGER THAN YOUR OLD ONES. HOW MANY DONUTS DID YOU EAT YESTERDAY?
AW, I ONLY --
RRRRIIPP!
⁝SIGH⁝ I GUESS I'LL JUST HAVE TO GO BUY THE NEXT SIZE UP. YOU HAVE TO HAVE SOMETHING TO WEAR TO WORK.
SOON...
HOMEY! I'M BACK WITH YOUR NEW PANTS!
HIGH & WIDE
HOMER?

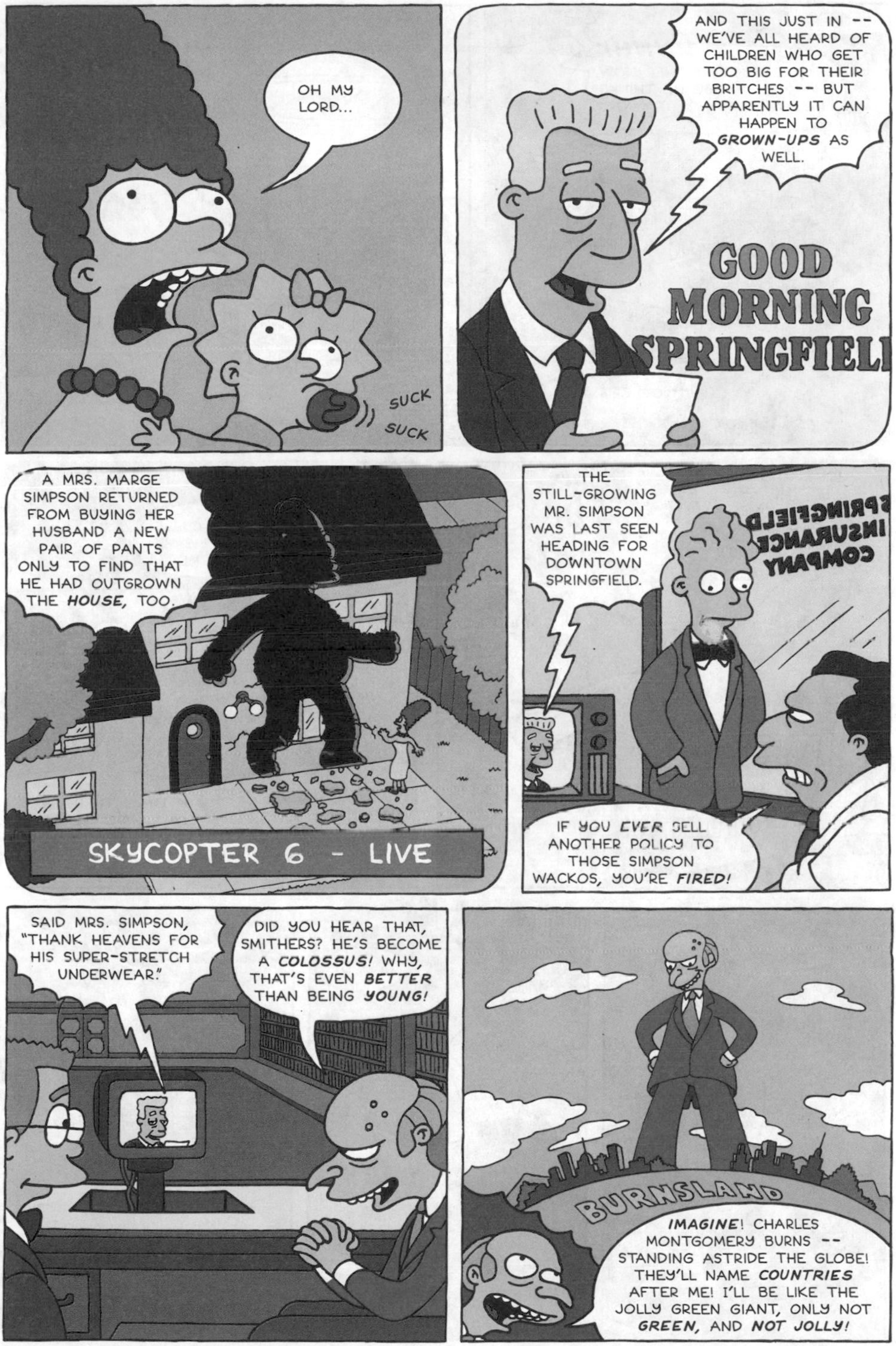
OH MY LORD...
SUCK SUCK
AND THIS JUST IN -- WE'VE ALL HEARD OF CHILDREN WHO GET TOO BIG FOR THEIR BRITCHES -- BUT APPARENTLY IT CAN HAPPEN TO GROWN-UPS AS WELL.
GOOD MORNING SPRINGFIEL
A MRS. MARGE SIMPSON RETURNED FROM BUYING HER HUSBAND A NEW PAIR OF PANTS ONLY TO FIND THAT HE HAD OUTGROWN THE HOUSE, TOO.
SKYCOPTER 6 - LIVE
THE STILL-GROWING MR. SIMPSON WAS LAST SEEN HEADING FOR DOWNTOWN SPRINGFIELD.
SPRINGFIELD INSURANCE COMPANY
IF YOU EVER SELL ANOTHER POLICY TO THOSE SIMPSON WACKOS, YOU'RE FIRED!
SAID MRS. SIMPSON, "THANK HEAVENS FOR HIS SUPER-STRETCH UNDERWEAR."
DID YOU HEAR THAT, SMITHERS? HE'S BECOME A COLOSSUS! WHY, THAT'S EVEN BETTER THAN BEING YOUNG!
BURNSLAND
IMAGINE! CHARLES MONTGOMERY BURNS -- STANDING ASTRIDE THE GLOBE! THEY'LL NAME COUNTRIES AFTER ME! I'LL BE LIKE THE JOLLY GREEN GIANT, ONLY NOT GREEN, AND NOT JOLLY!

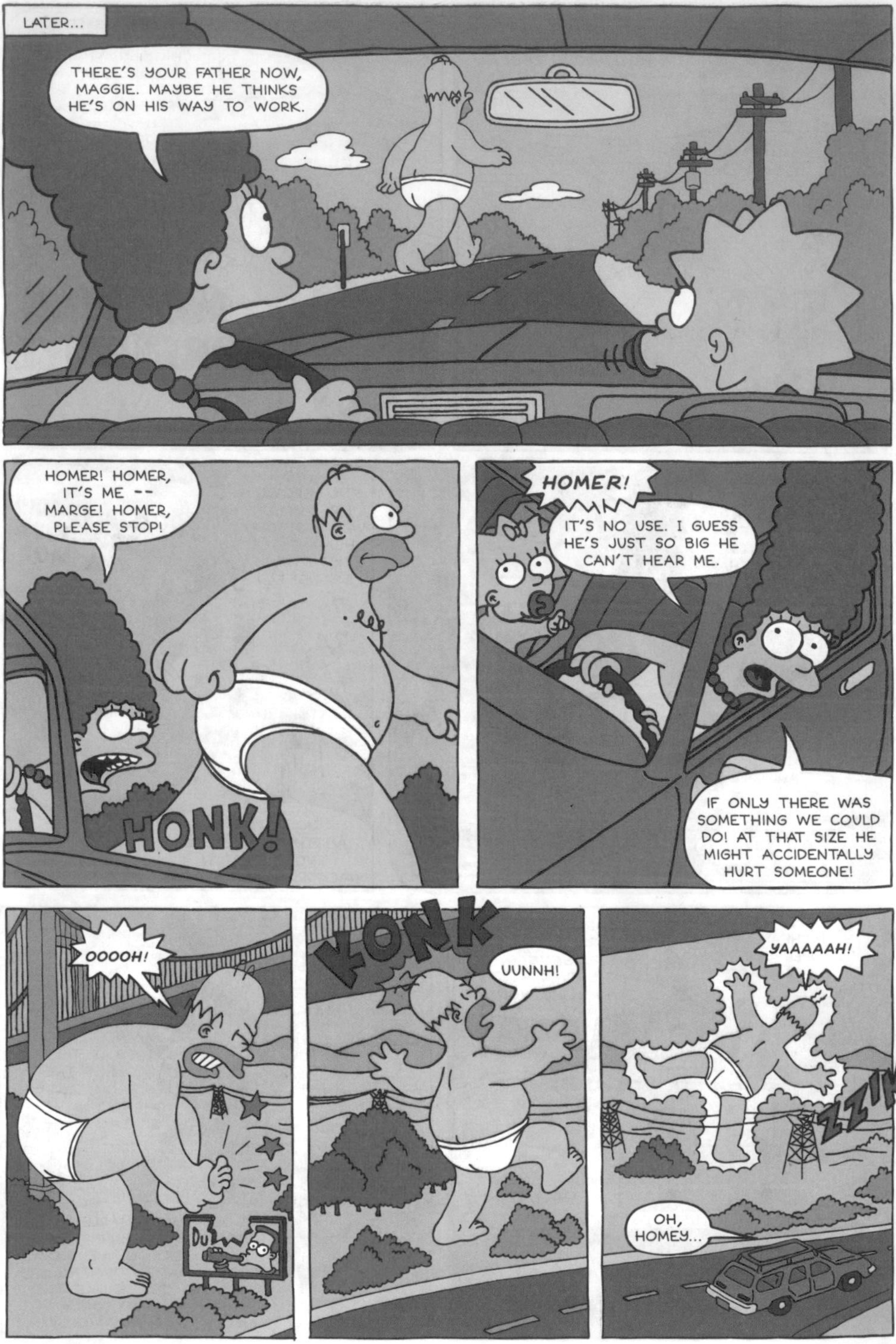
LATER...
THERE'S YOUR FATHER NOW, MAGGIE. MAYBE HE THINKS HE'S ON HIS WAY TO WORK.
HOMER! HOMER, IT'S ME -- MARGE! HOMER, PLEASE STOP!
HONK!
HOMER!
IT'S NO USE. I GUESS HE'S JUST SO BIG HE CAN'T HEAR ME.
IF ONLY THERE WAS SOMETHING WE COULD DO! AT THAT SIZE HE MIGHT ACCIDENTALLY HURT SOMEONE!
OOOOH!
KONK
UUNNH!
YAAAAAH!
ZZZIK!
OH, HOMEY...

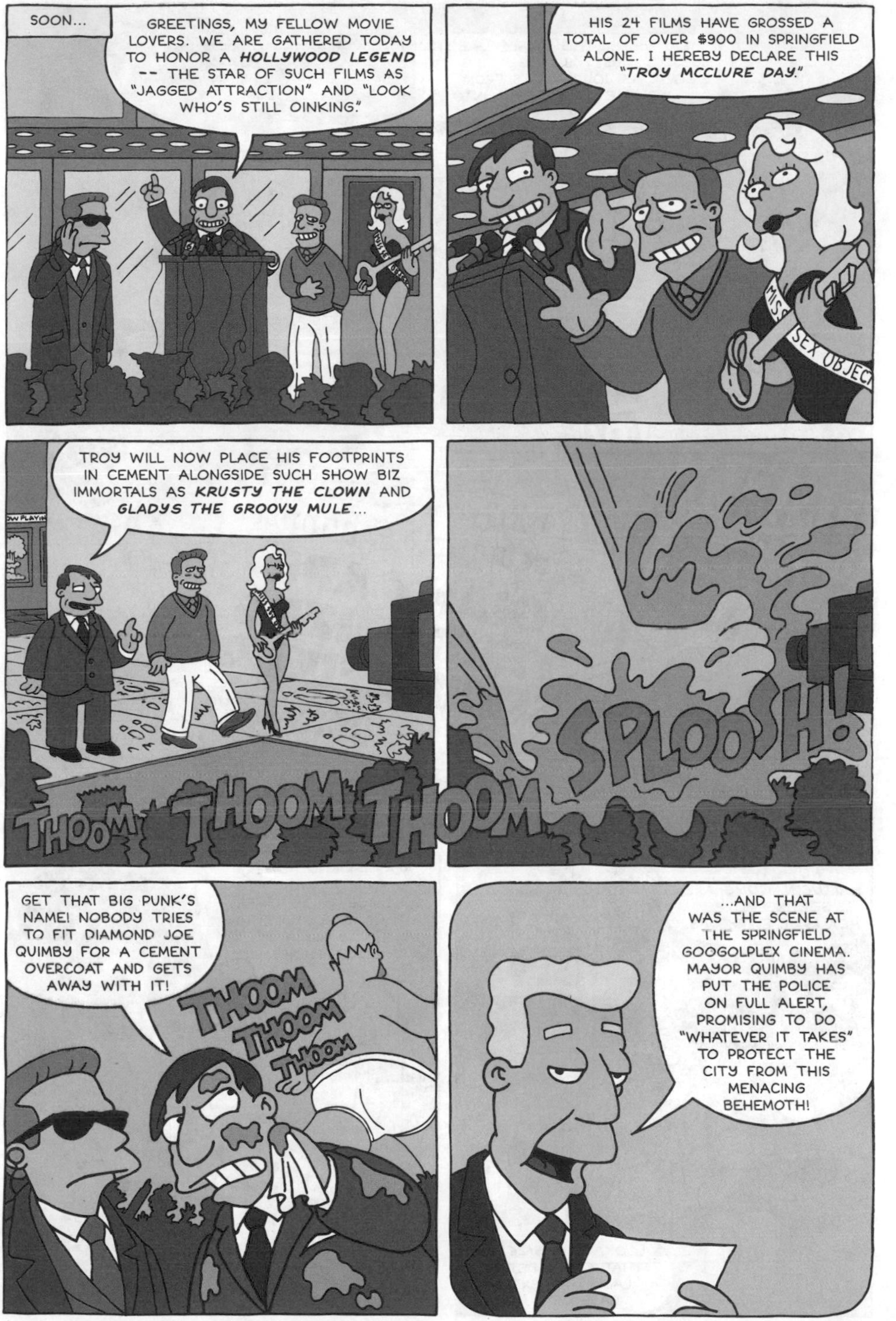
SOON...
GREETINGS, MY FELLOW MOVIE LOVERS. WE ARE GATHERED TODAY TO HONOR A **HOLLYWOOD LEGEND** -- THE STAR OF SUCH FILMS AS "JAGGED ATTRACTION" AND "LOOK WHO'S STILL OINKING."
HIS 24 FILMS HAVE GROSSED A TOTAL OF OVER $900 IN SPRINGFIELD ALONE. I HEREBY DECLARE THIS "**TROY MCCLURE DAY.**"
MISS SEX OBJECT
TROY WILL NOW PLACE HIS FOOTPRINTS IN CEMENT ALONGSIDE SUCH SHOW BIZ IMMORTALS AS **KRUSTY THE CLOWN** AND **GLADYS THE GROOVY MULE**...
THOOM THOOM THOOM
SPLOOSH!
GET THAT BIG PUNK'S NAME! NOBODY TRIES TO FIT DIAMOND JOE QUIMBY FOR A CEMENT OVERCOAT AND GETS AWAY WITH IT!
THOOM THOOM THOOM
...AND THAT WAS THE SCENE AT THE SPRINGFIELD GOOGOLPLEX CINEMA. MAYOR QUIMBY HAS PUT THE POLICE ON FULL ALERT, PROMISING TO DO "WHATEVER IT TAKES" TO PROTECT THE CITY FROM THIS MENACING BEHEMOTH!

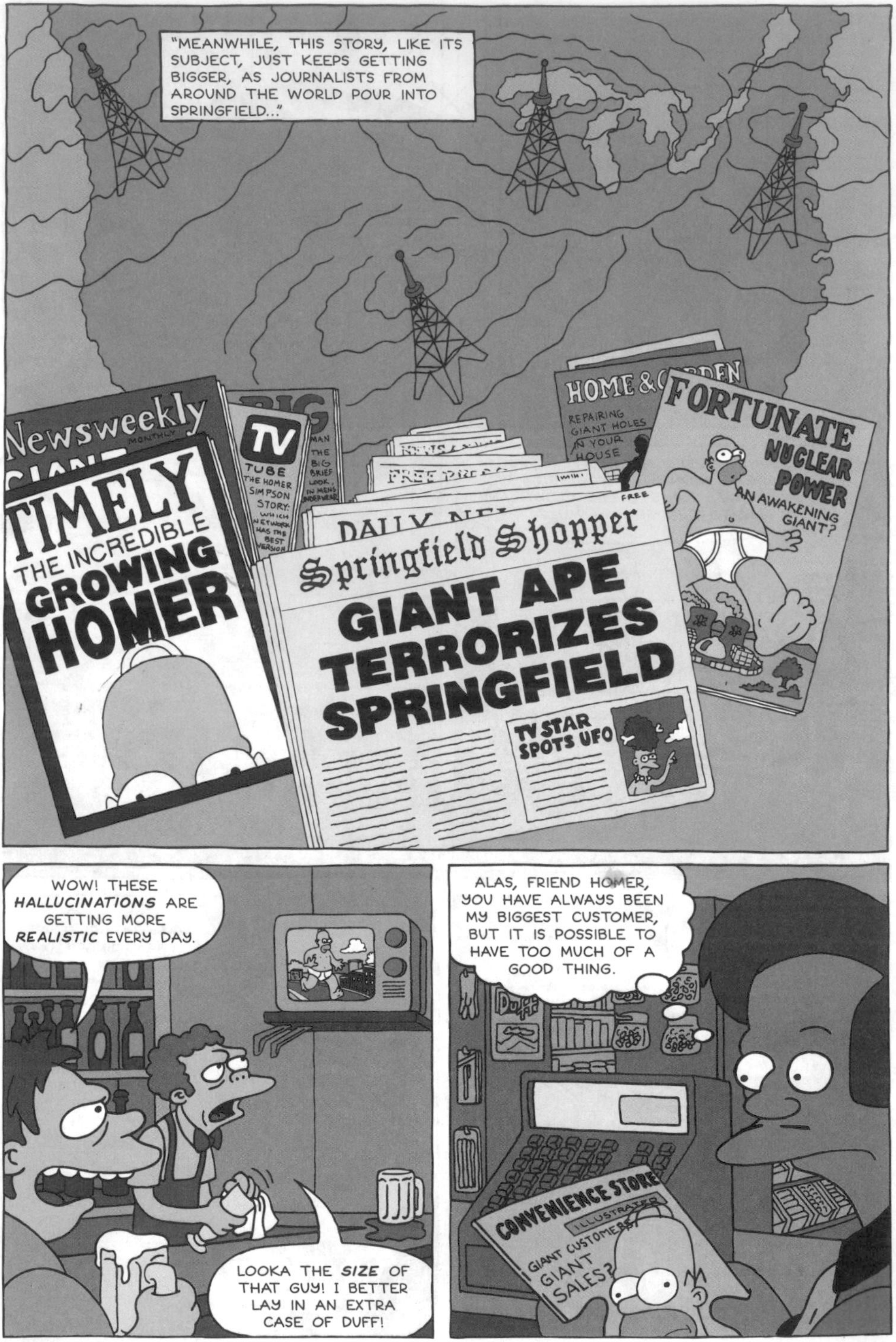

"MEANWHILE, THIS STORY, LIKE ITS SUBJECT, JUST KEEPS GETTING BIGGER, AS JOURNALISTS FROM AROUND THE WORLD POUR INTO SPRINGFIELD..."
Newsweekly
TIMELY
THE INCREDIBLE GROWING HOMER
TV
HOME & GARDEN
REPAIRING GIANT HOLES IN YOUR HOUSE
FORTUNATE
NUCLEAR POWER
AN AWAKENING GIANT?
FREE
Springfield Shopper
GIANT APE TERRORIZES SPRINGFIELD
TV STAR SPOTS UFO
WOW! THESE *HALLUCINATIONS* ARE GETTING MORE *REALISTIC* EVERY DAY.
LOOKA THE *SIZE* OF THAT GUY! I BETTER LAY IN AN EXTRA CASE OF DUFF!
ALAS, FRIEND HOMER, YOU HAVE ALWAYS BEEN MY BIGGEST CUSTOMER, BUT IT IS POSSIBLE TO HAVE TOO MUCH OF A GOOD THING.
CONVENIENCE STORE
ILLUSTRATED
GIANT CUSTOMERS, GIANT SALES?

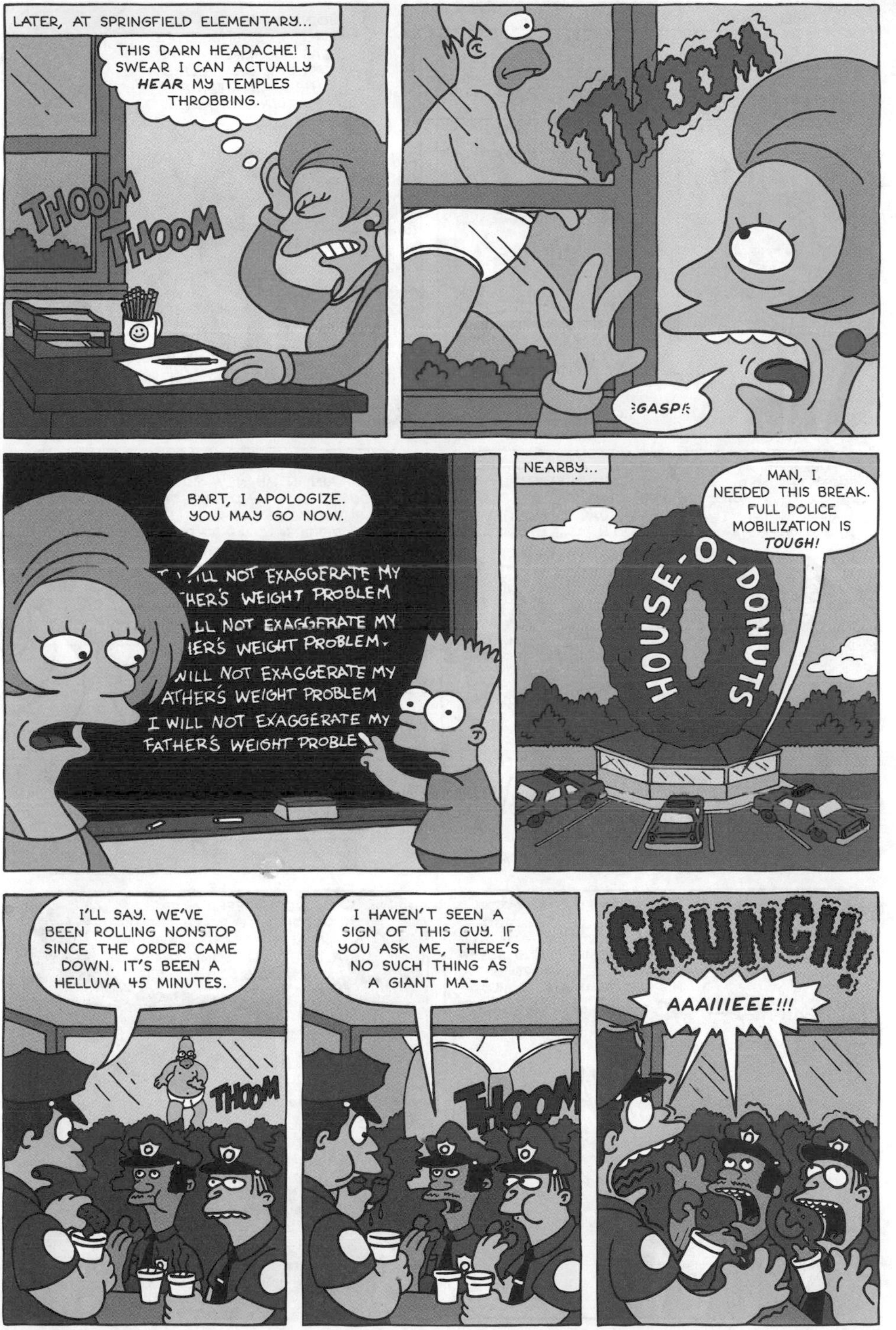

LATER, AT SPRINGFIELD ELEMENTARY...
THIS DARN HEADACHE! I SWEAR I CAN ACTUALLY HEAR MY TEMPLES THROBBING.
THOOM
THOOM
THOOM
GASP!
BART, I APOLOGIZE. YOU MAY GO NOW.
I WILL NOT EXAGGERATE MY FATHER'S WEIGHT PROBLEM
NEARBY...
MAN, I NEEDED THIS BREAK. FULL POLICE MOBILIZATION IS TOUGH!
HOUSE-O-DONUTS
I'LL SAY. WE'VE BEEN ROLLING NONSTOP SINCE THE ORDER CAME DOWN. IT'S BEEN A HELLUVA 45 MINUTES.
THOOM
I HAVEN'T SEEN A SIGN OF THIS GUY. IF YOU ASK ME, THERE'S NO SUCH THING AS A GIANT MA--
THOOM
CRUNCH!
AAAIIIEEE!!!

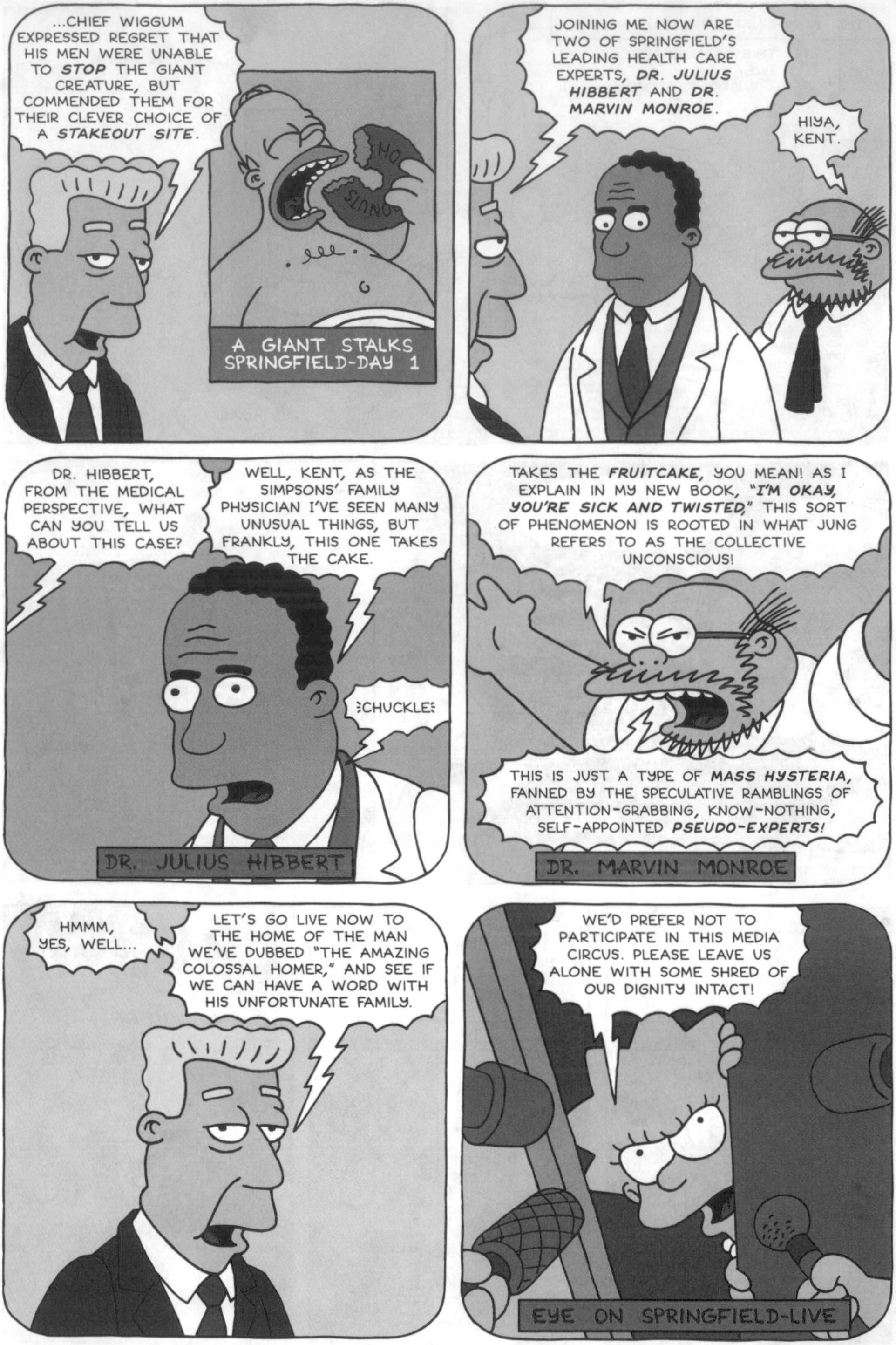
...CHIEF WIGGUM EXPRESSED REGRET THAT HIS MEN WERE UNABLE TO STOP THE GIANT CREATURE, BUT COMMENDED THEM FOR THEIR CLEVER CHOICE OF A STAKEOUT SITE.
A GIANT STALKS SPRINGFIELD-DAY 1
JOINING ME NOW ARE TWO OF SPRINGFIELD'S LEADING HEALTH CARE EXPERTS, DR. JULIUS HIBBERT AND DR. MARVIN MONROE.
HIYA, KENT.
DR. HIBBERT, FROM THE MEDICAL PERSPECTIVE, WHAT CAN YOU TELL US ABOUT THIS CASE?
WELL, KENT, AS THE SIMPSONS' FAMILY PHYSICIAN I'VE SEEN MANY UNUSUAL THINGS, BUT FRANKLY, THIS ONE TAKES THE CAKE.
CHUCKLE
DR. JULIUS HIBBERT
TAKES THE FRUITCAKE, YOU MEAN! AS I EXPLAIN IN MY NEW BOOK, "I'M OKAY, YOU'RE SICK AND TWISTED," THIS SORT OF PHENOMENON IS ROOTED IN WHAT JUNG REFERS TO AS THE COLLECTIVE UNCONSCIOUS!
THIS IS JUST A TYPE OF MASS HYSTERIA, FANNED BY THE SPECULATIVE RAMBLINGS OF ATTENTION-GRABBING, KNOW-NOTHING, SELF-APPOINTED PSEUDO-EXPERTS!
DR. MARVIN MONROE
HMMM, YES, WELL...
LET'S GO LIVE NOW TO THE HOME OF THE MAN WE'VE DUBBED "THE AMAZING COLOSSAL HOMER," AND SEE IF WE CAN HAVE A WORD WITH HIS UNFORTUNATE FAMILY.
WE'D PREFER NOT TO PARTICIPATE IN THIS MEDIA CIRCUS. PLEASE LEAVE US ALONE WITH SOME SHRED OF OUR DIGNITY INTACT!
EYE ON SPRINGFIELD-LIVE

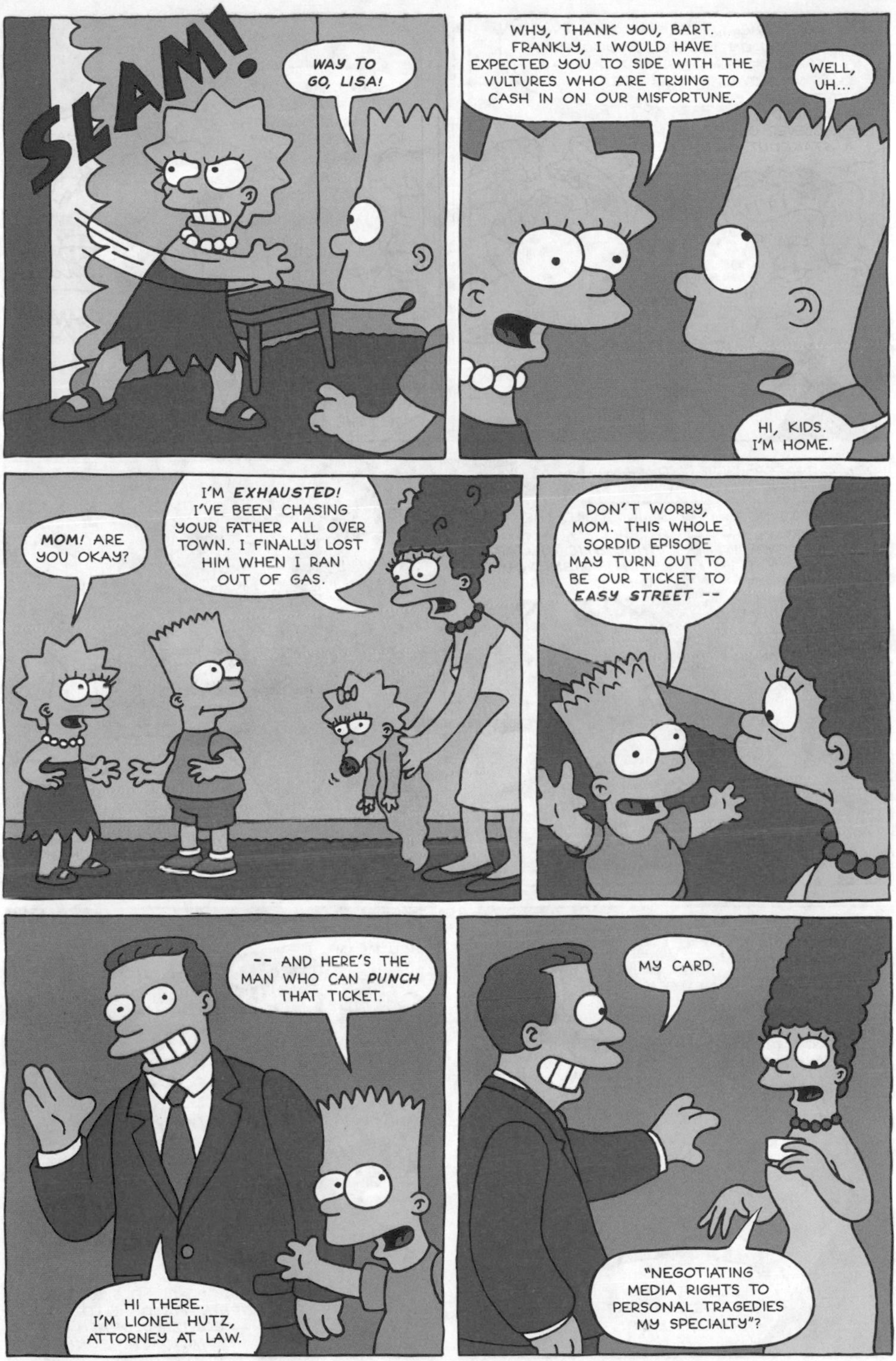
SLAM!
WAY TO GO, LISA!
WHY, THANK YOU, BART. FRANKLY, I WOULD HAVE EXPECTED YOU TO SIDE WITH THE VULTURES WHO ARE TRYING TO CASH IN ON OUR MISFORTUNE.
WELL, UH...
HI, KIDS. I'M HOME.
MOM! ARE YOU OKAY?
I'M EXHAUSTED! I'VE BEEN CHASING YOUR FATHER ALL OVER TOWN. I FINALLY LOST HIM WHEN I RAN OUT OF GAS.
DON'T WORRY, MOM. THIS WHOLE SORDID EPISODE MAY TURN OUT TO BE OUR TICKET TO EASY STREET --
-- AND HERE'S THE MAN WHO CAN PUNCH THAT TICKET.
HI THERE. I'M LIONEL HUTZ, ATTORNEY AT LAW.
MY CARD.
"NEGOTIATING MEDIA RIGHTS TO PERSONAL TRAGEDIES MY SPECIALTY"?

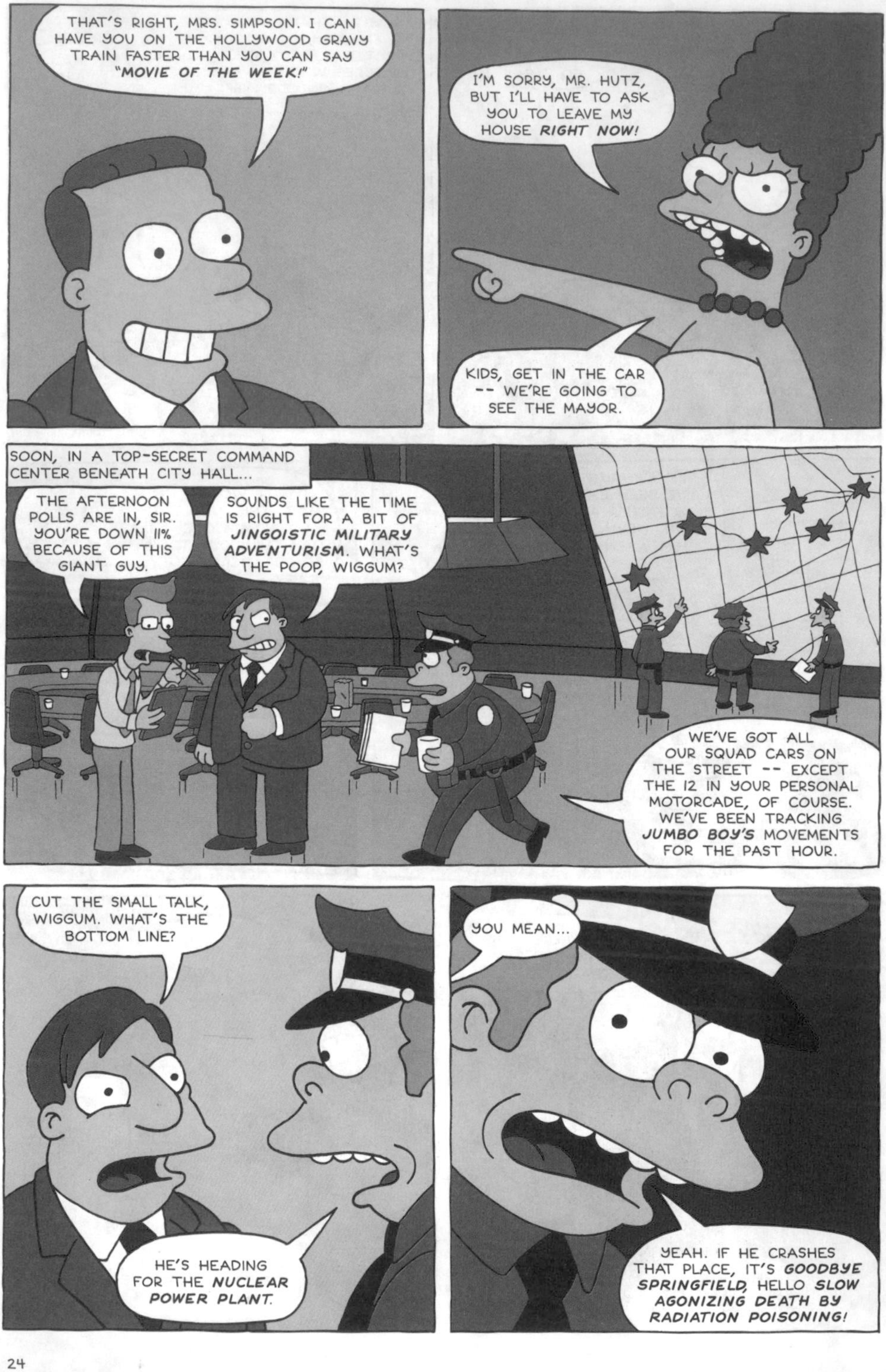
THAT'S RIGHT, MRS. SIMPSON. I CAN HAVE YOU ON THE HOLLYWOOD GRAVY TRAIN FASTER THAN YOU CAN SAY "MOVIE OF THE WEEK!"
I'M SORRY, MR. HUTZ, BUT I'LL HAVE TO ASK YOU TO LEAVE MY HOUSE RIGHT NOW!
KIDS, GET IN THE CAR -- WE'RE GOING TO SEE THE MAYOR.
SOON, IN A TOP-SECRET COMMAND CENTER BENEATH CITY HALL...
THE AFTERNOON POLLS ARE IN, SIR. YOU'RE DOWN 11% BECAUSE OF THIS GIANT GUY.
SOUNDS LIKE THE TIME IS RIGHT FOR A BIT OF JINGOISTIC MILITARY ADVENTURISM. WHAT'S THE POOP, WIGGUM?
WE'VE GOT ALL OUR SQUAD CARS ON THE STREET -- EXCEPT THE 12 IN YOUR PERSONAL MOTORCADE, OF COURSE. WE'VE BEEN TRACKING JUMBO BOY'S MOVEMENTS FOR THE PAST HOUR.
CUT THE SMALL TALK, WIGGUM. WHAT'S THE BOTTOM LINE?
HE'S HEADING FOR THE NUCLEAR POWER PLANT.
YOU MEAN...
YEAH. IF HE CRASHES THAT PLACE, IT'S GOODBYE SPRINGFIELD, HELLO SLOW AGONIZING DEATH BY RADIATION POISONING!

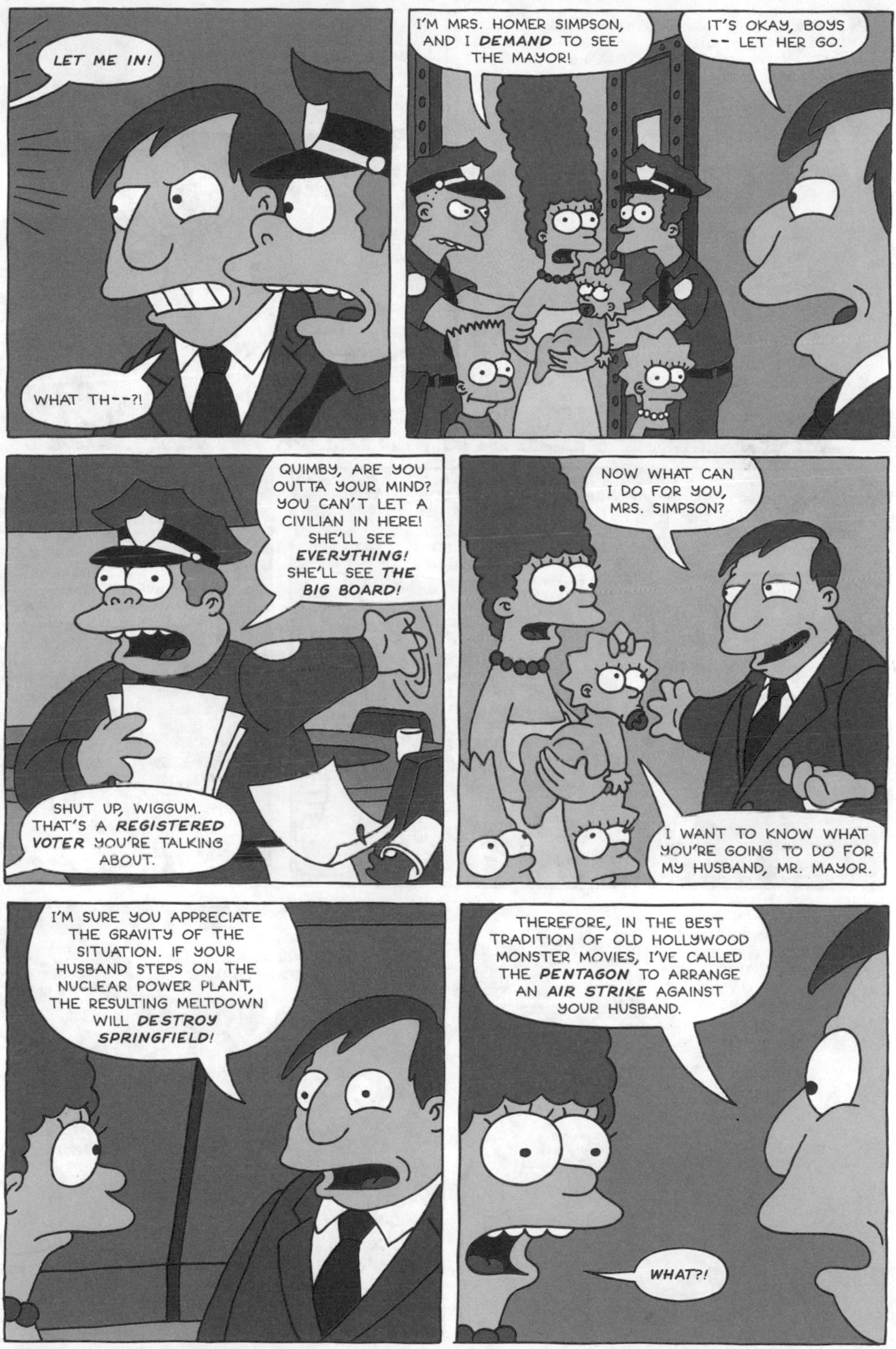
LET ME IN!
WHAT TH--?!
I'M MRS. HOMER SIMPSON, AND I DEMAND TO SEE THE MAYOR!
IT'S OKAY, BOYS -- LET HER GO.
QUIMBY, ARE YOU OUTTA YOUR MIND? YOU CAN'T LET A CIVILIAN IN HERE! SHE'LL SEE EVERYTHING! SHE'LL SEE THE BIG BOARD!
SHUT UP, WIGGUM. THAT'S A REGISTERED VOTER YOU'RE TALKING ABOUT.
NOW WHAT CAN I DO FOR YOU, MRS. SIMPSON?
I WANT TO KNOW WHAT YOU'RE GOING TO DO FOR MY HUSBAND, MR. MAYOR.
I'M SURE YOU APPRECIATE THE GRAVITY OF THE SITUATION. IF YOUR HUSBAND STEPS ON THE NUCLEAR POWER PLANT, THE RESULTING MELTDOWN WILL DESTROY SPRINGFIELD!
THEREFORE, IN THE BEST TRADITION OF OLD HOLLYWOOD MONSTER MOVIES, I'VE CALLED THE PENTAGON TO ARRANGE AN AIR STRIKE AGAINST YOUR HUSBAND.
WHAT?!

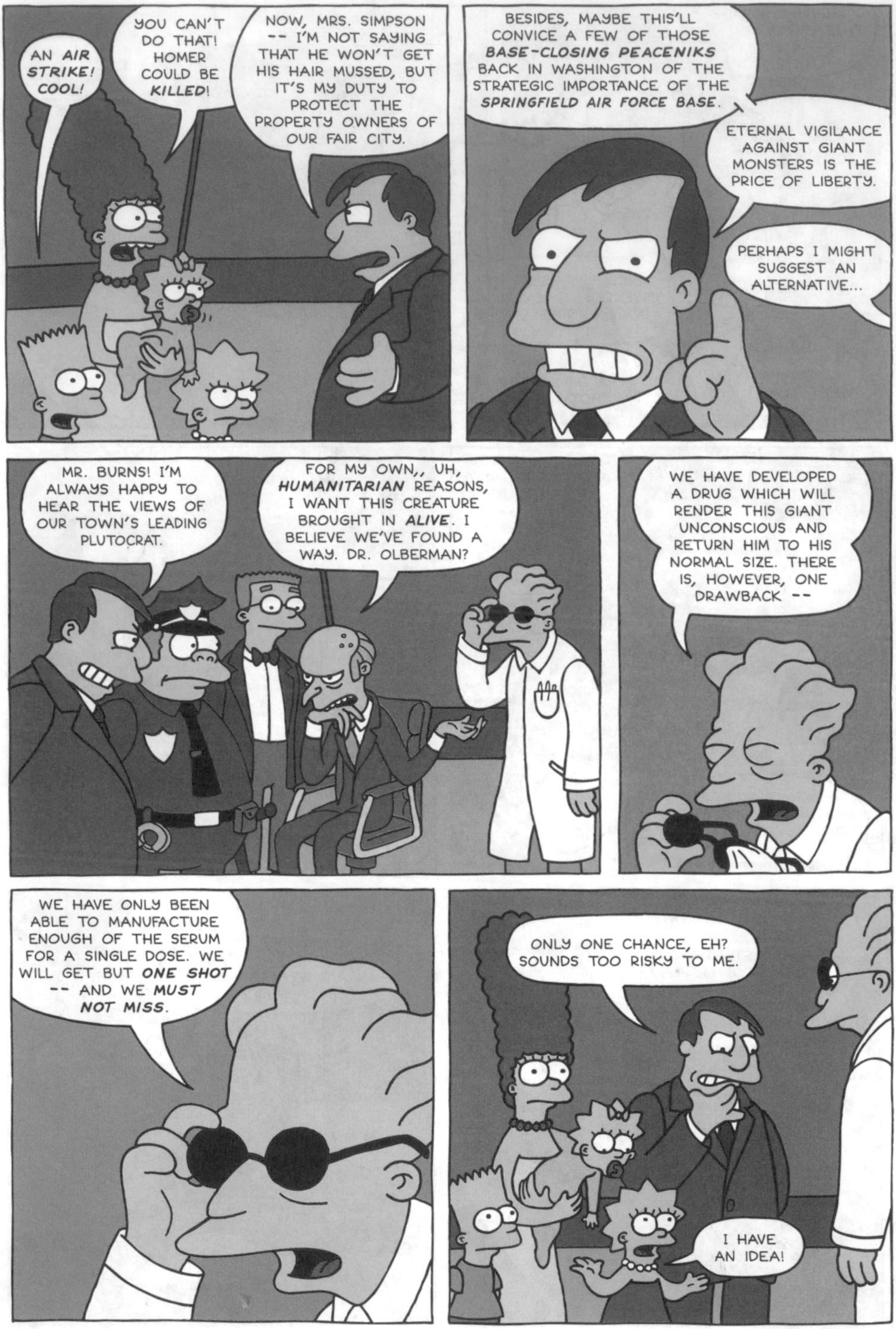
AN AIR STRIKE! COOL!
YOU CAN'T DO THAT! HOMER COULD BE KILLED!
NOW, MRS. SIMPSON -- I'M NOT SAYING THAT HE WON'T GET HIS HAIR MUSSED, BUT IT'S MY DUTY TO PROTECT THE PROPERTY OWNERS OF OUR FAIR CITY.
BESIDES, MAYBE THIS'LL CONVICE A FEW OF THOSE BASE-CLOSING PEACENIKS BACK IN WASHINGTON OF THE STRATEGIC IMPORTANCE OF THE SPRINGFIELD AIR FORCE BASE.
ETERNAL VIGILANCE AGAINST GIANT MONSTERS IS THE PRICE OF LIBERTY.
PERHAPS I MIGHT SUGGEST AN ALTERNATIVE...
MR. BURNS! I'M ALWAYS HAPPY TO HEAR THE VIEWS OF OUR TOWN'S LEADING PLUTOCRAT.
FOR MY OWN,, UH, HUMANITARIAN REASONS, I WANT THIS CREATURE BROUGHT IN ALIVE. I BELIEVE WE'VE FOUND A WAY. DR. OLBERMAN?
WE HAVE DEVELOPED A DRUG WHICH WILL RENDER THIS GIANT UNCONSCIOUS AND RETURN HIM TO HIS NORMAL SIZE. THERE IS, HOWEVER, ONE DRAWBACK --
WE HAVE ONLY BEEN ABLE TO MANUFACTURE ENOUGH OF THE SERUM FOR A SINGLE DOSE. WE WILL GET BUT ONE SHOT -- AND WE MUST NOT MISS.
ONLY ONE CHANCE, EH? SOUNDS TOO RISKY TO ME.
I HAVE AN IDEA!

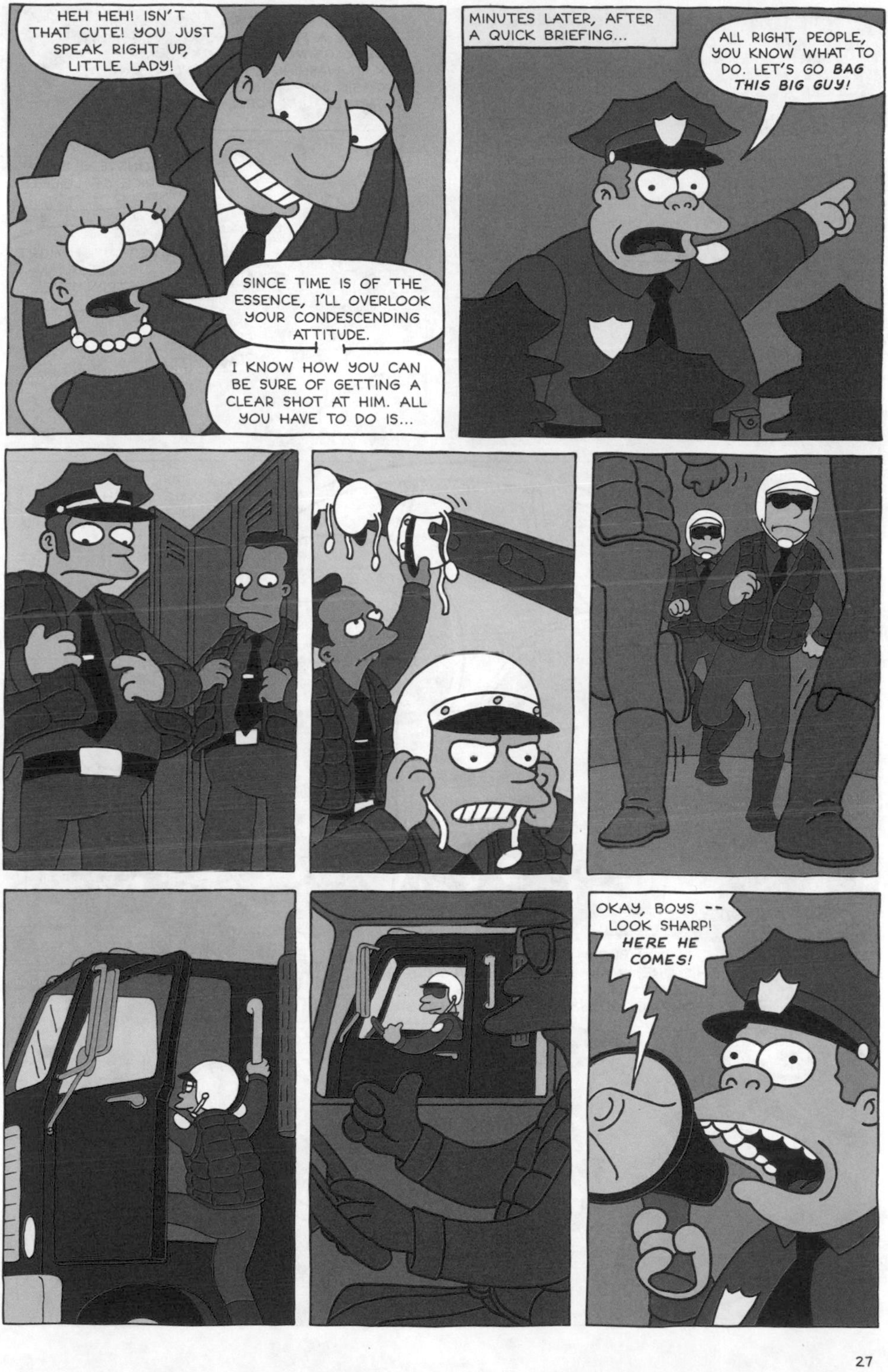
HEH HEH! ISN'T THAT CUTE! YOU JUST SPEAK RIGHT UP, LITTLE LADY!
SINCE TIME IS OF THE ESSENCE, I'LL OVERLOOK YOUR CONDESCENDING ATTITUDE.
I KNOW HOW YOU CAN BE SURE OF GETTING A CLEAR SHOT AT HIM. ALL YOU HAVE TO DO IS...
MINUTES LATER, AFTER A QUICK BRIEFING...
ALL RIGHT, PEOPLE, YOU KNOW WHAT TO DO. LET'S GO BAG THIS BIG GUY!
OKAY, BOYS -- LOOK SHARP! HERE HE COMES!

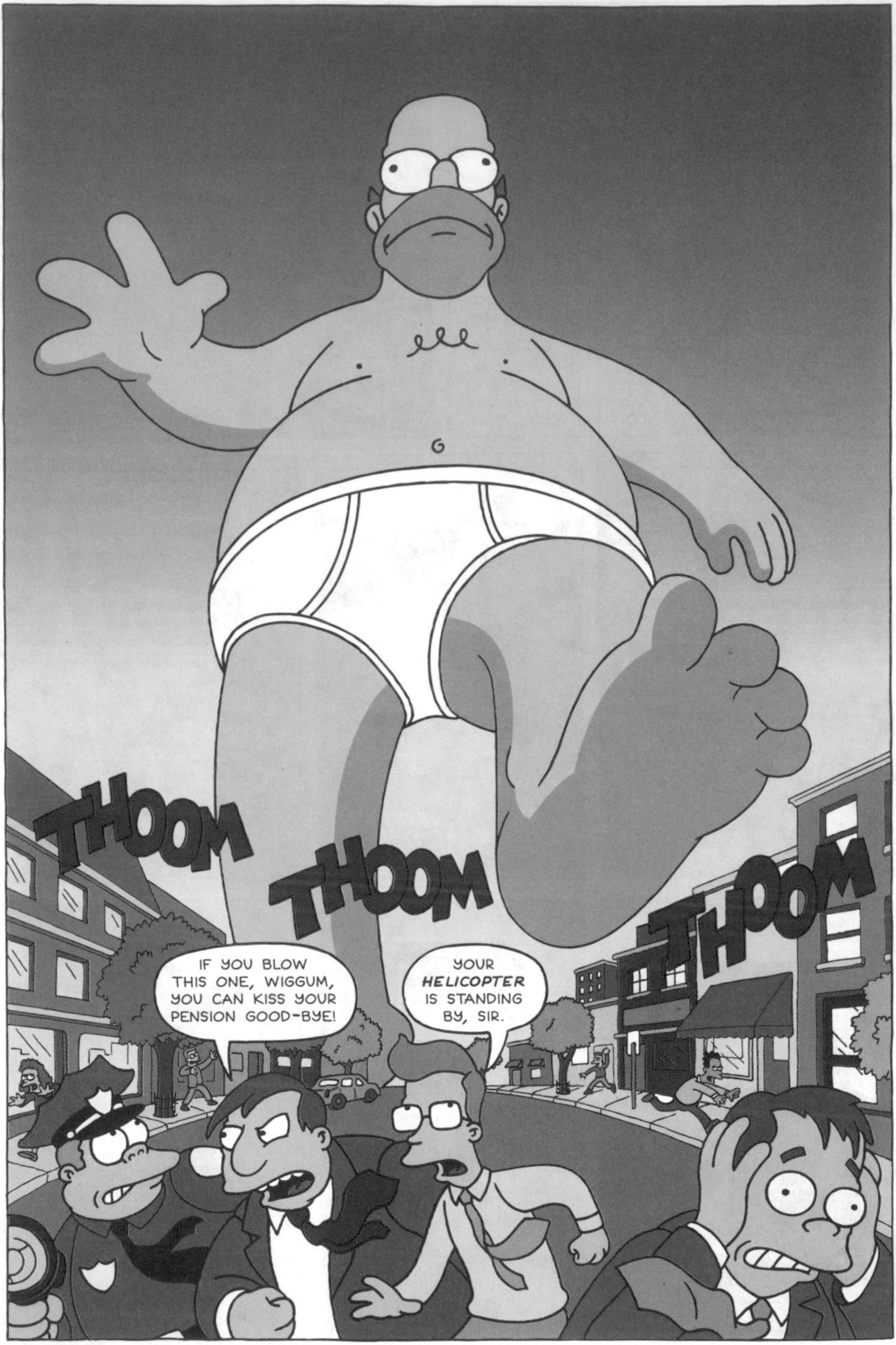
THOOM
THOOM
THOOM
IF YOU BLOW THIS ONE, WIGGUM, YOU CAN KISS YOUR PENSION GOOD-BYE!
YOUR HELICOPTER IS STANDING BY, SIR.

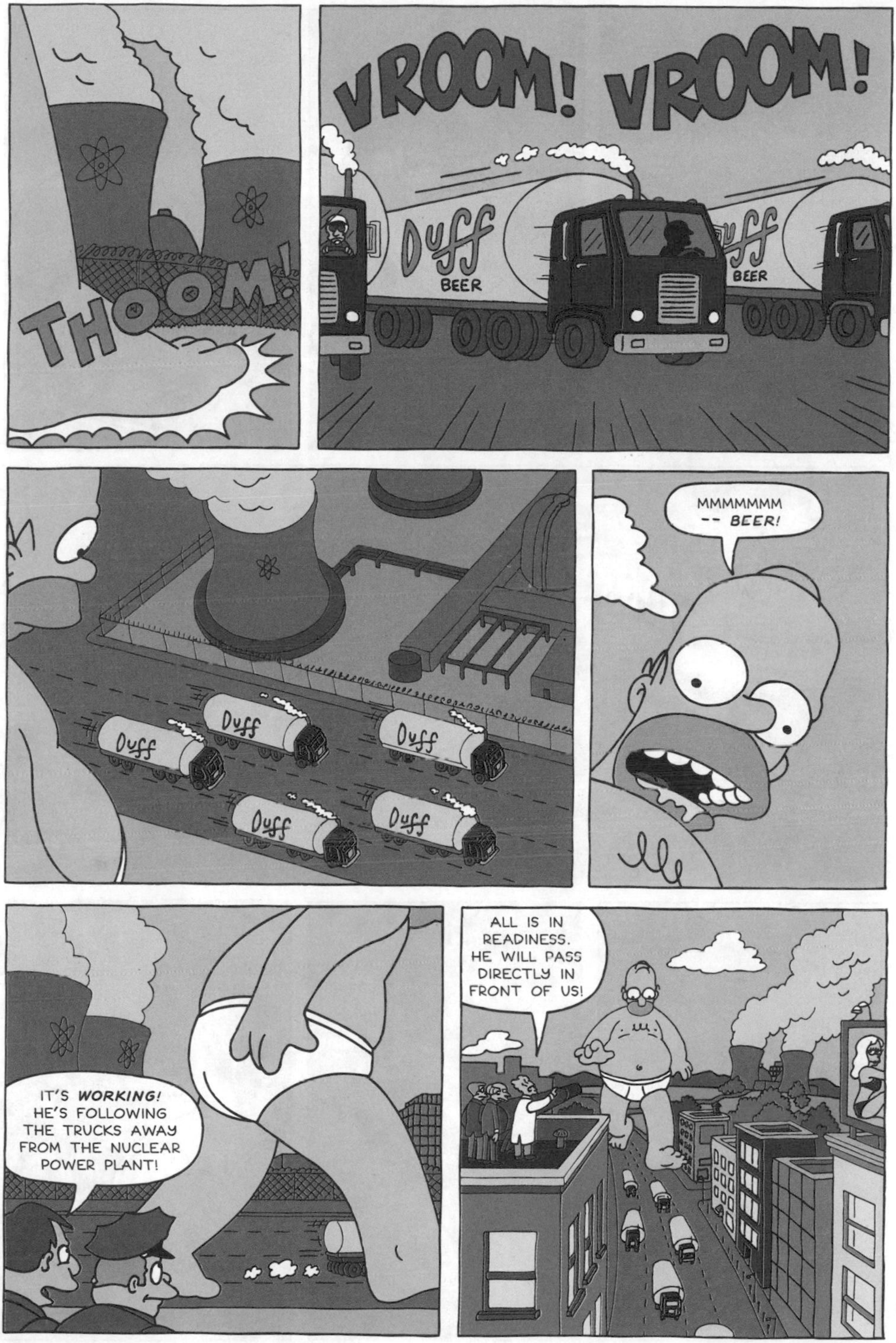
THOOM!
VROOM! VROOM!
DUFF BEER
DUFF BEER
MMMMMMM -- BEER!
IT'S WORKING! HE'S FOLLOWING THE TRUCKS AWAY FROM THE NUCLEAR POWER PLANT!
ALL IS IN READINESS. HE WILL PASS DIRECTLY IN FRONT OF US!

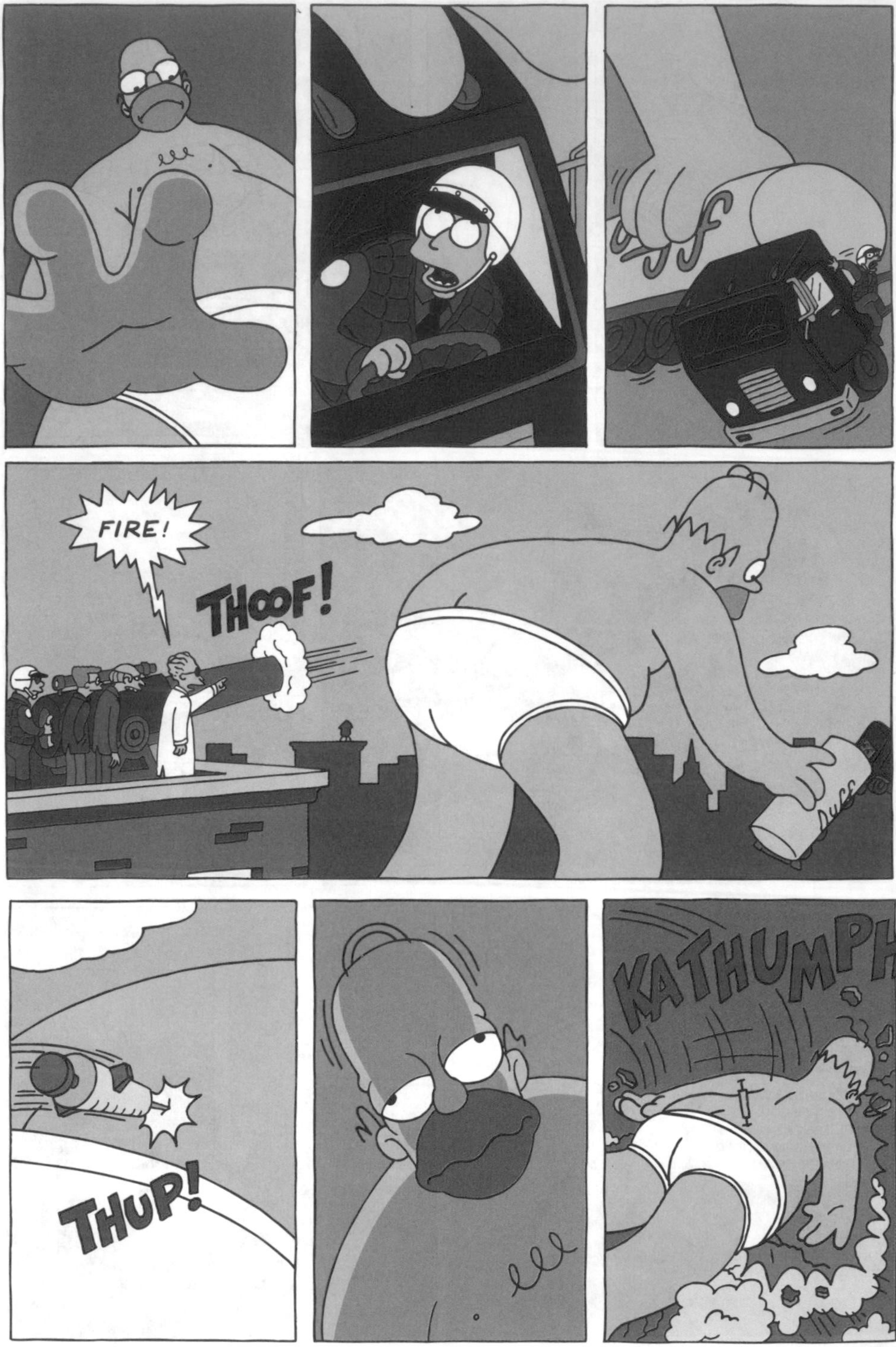

DUFF
FIRE!
THOOF!
DUFF
THUP!
KATHUMPH

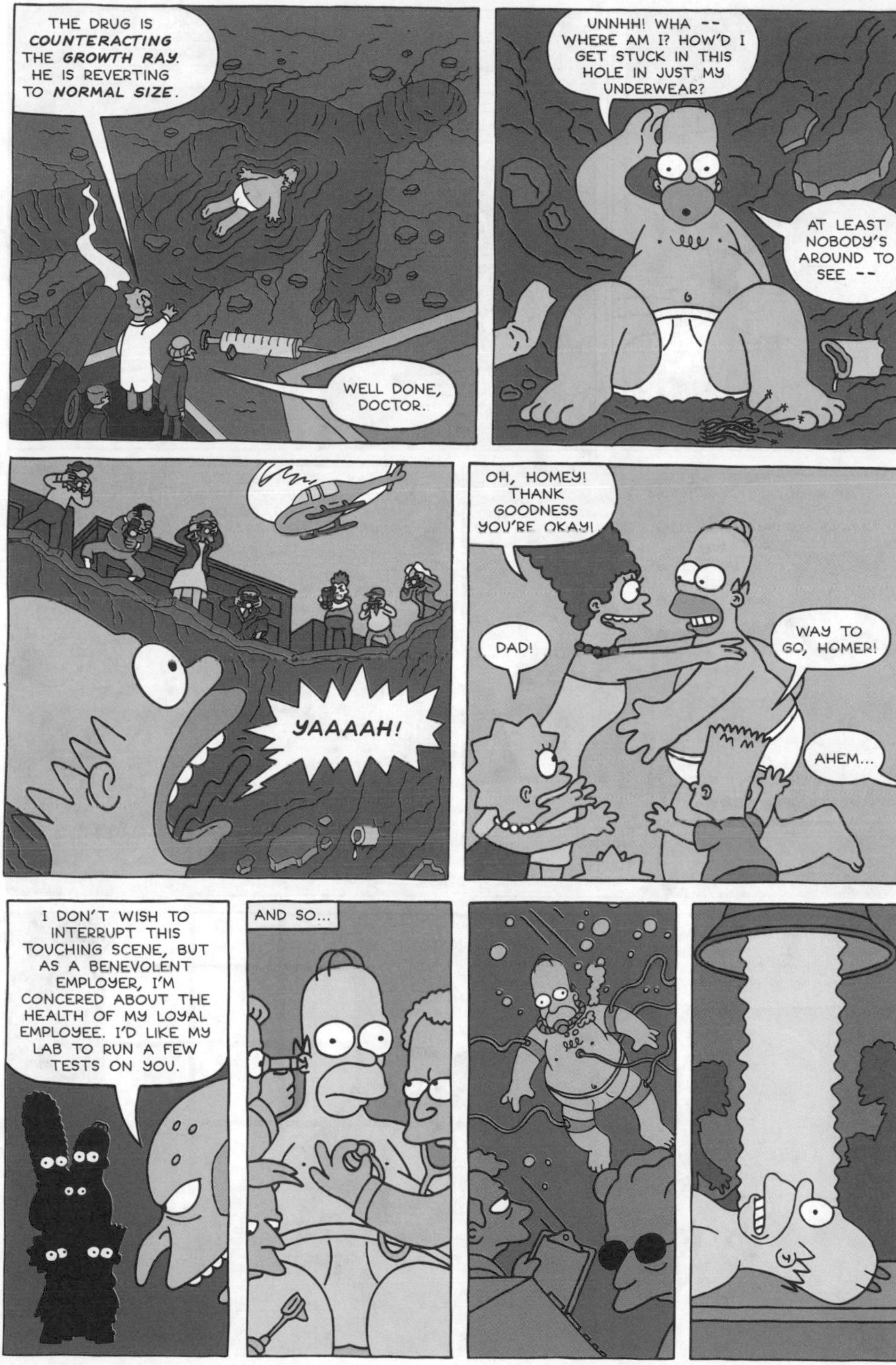
THE DRUG IS *COUNTERACTING* THE *GROWTH RAY*. HE IS REVERTING TO *NORMAL SIZE*.
WELL DONE, DOCTOR.
UNNHH! WHA -- WHERE AM I? HOW'D I GET STUCK IN THIS HOLE IN JUST MY UNDERWEAR?
AT LEAST NOBODY'S AROUND TO SEE --
YAAAAH!
OH, HOMEY! THANK GOODNESS YOU'RE OKAY!
DAD!
WAY TO GO, HOMER!
AHEM...
I DON'T WISH TO INTERRUPT THIS TOUCHING SCENE, BUT AS A BENEVOLENT EMPLOYER, I'M CONCERED ABOUT THE HEALTH OF MY LOYAL EMPLOYEE. I'D LIKE MY LAB TO RUN A FEW TESTS ON YOU.
AND SO...

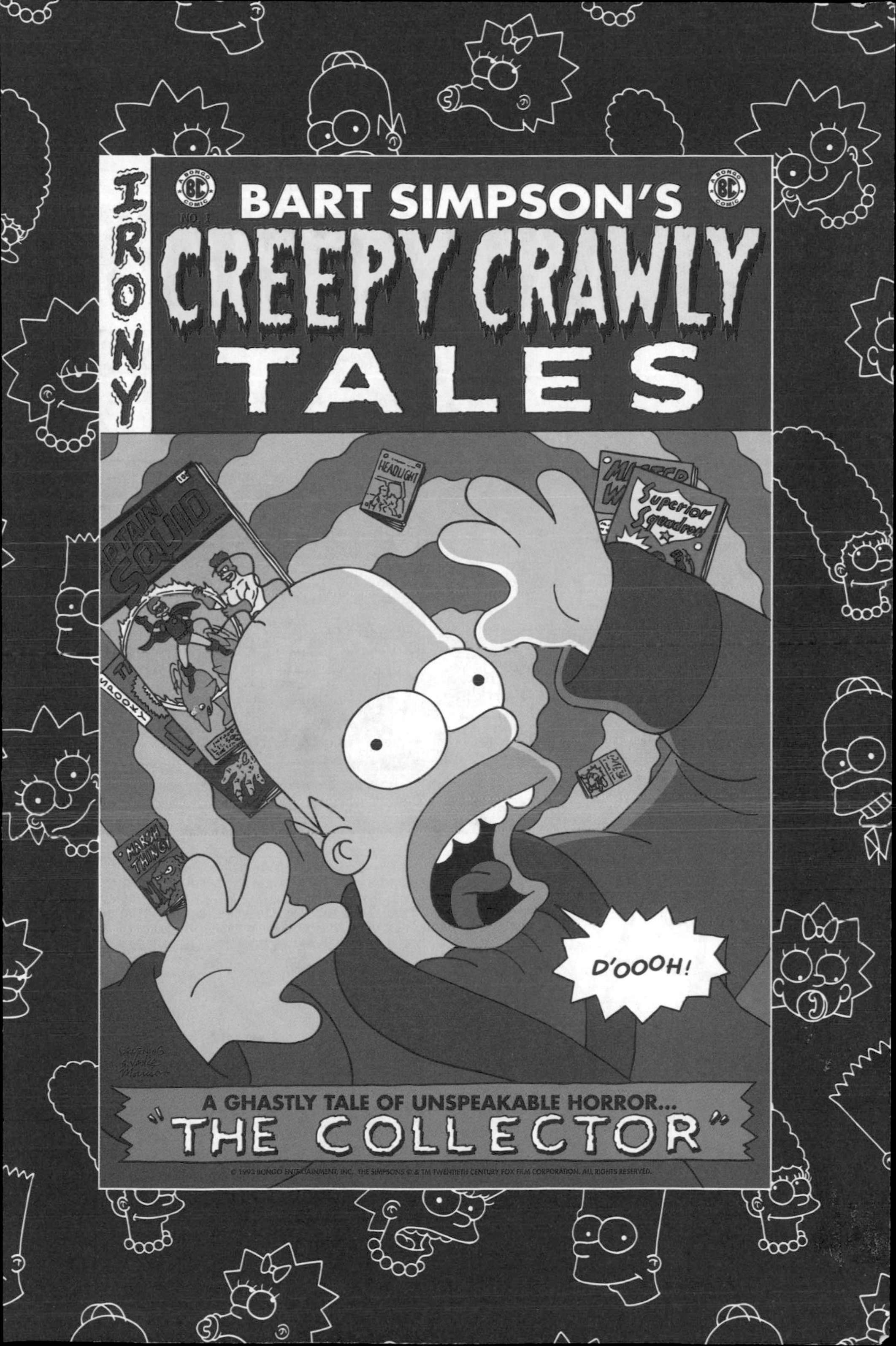
IRONY
BART SIMPSON'S
CREEPY CRAWLY TALES
A BONGO COMIC
BC
NO. 1
CAPTAIN SQUID
HEADLIGHT
Superior Squadron
MARSH THING!
D'OOOH!
A GHASTLY TALE OF UNSPEAKABLE HORROR...
"THE COLLECTOR"
© 1993 BONGO ENTERTAINMENT, INC. THE SIMPSONS © & TM TWENTIETH CENTURY FOX FILM CORPORATION. ALL RIGHTS RESERVED.

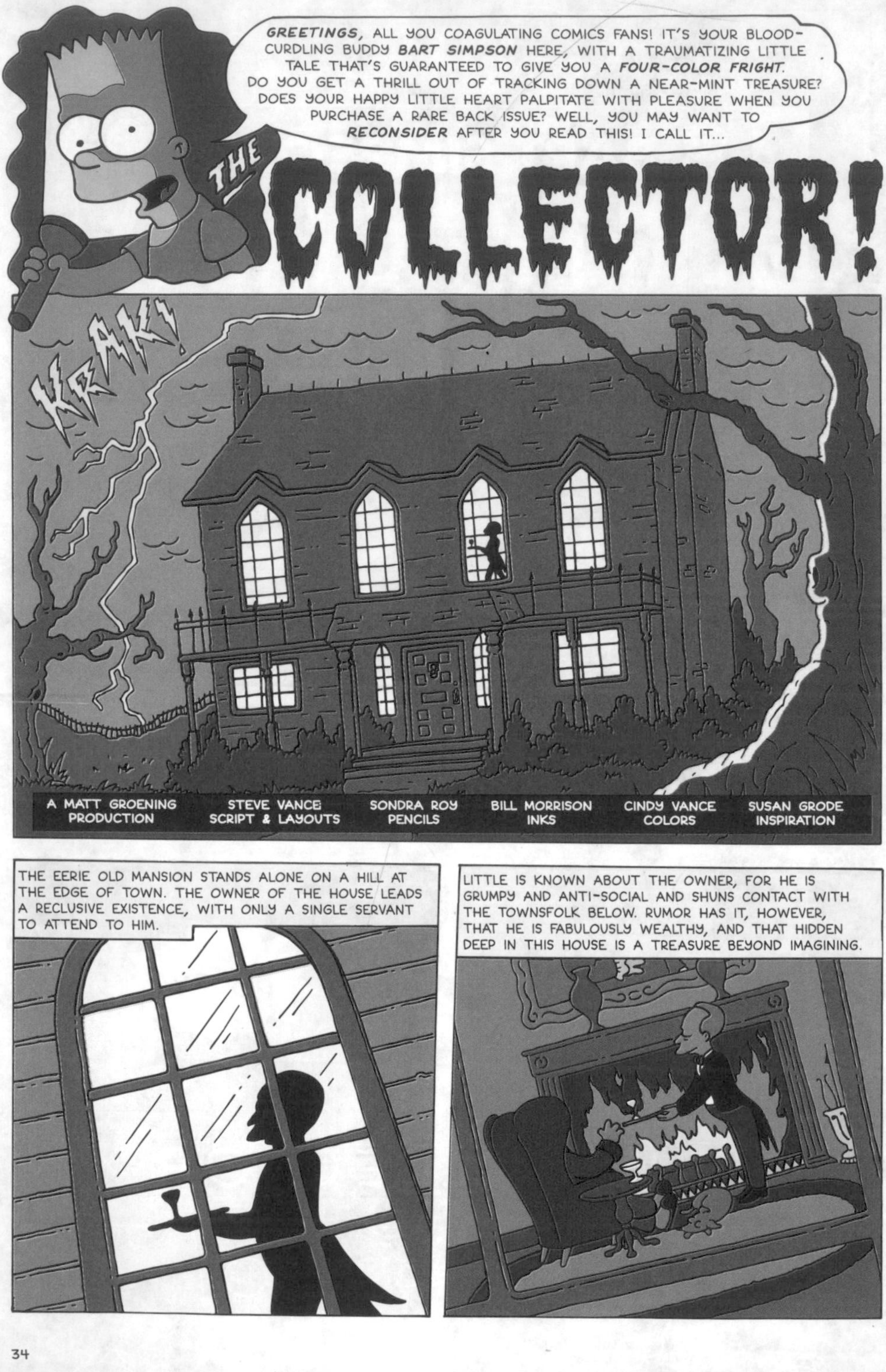
GREETINGS, ALL YOU COAGULATING COMICS FANS! IT'S YOUR BLOOD-CURDLING BUDDY BART SIMPSON HERE, WITH A TRAUMATIZING LITTLE TALE THAT'S GUARANTEED TO GIVE YOU A FOUR-COLOR FRIGHT. DO YOU GET A THRILL OUT OF TRACKING DOWN A NEAR-MINT TREASURE? DOES YOUR HAPPY LITTLE HEART PALPITATE WITH PLEASURE WHEN YOU PURCHASE A RARE BACK ISSUE? WELL, YOU MAY WANT TO RECONSIDER AFTER YOU READ THIS! I CALL IT...
THE COLLECTOR!
KRAK!
A MATT GROENING PRODUCTION
STEVE VANCE SCRIPT & LAYOUTS
SONDRA ROY PENCILS
BILL MORRISON INKS
CINDY VANCE COLORS
SUSAN GRODE INSPIRATION
THE EERIE OLD MANSION STANDS ALONE ON A HILL AT THE EDGE OF TOWN. THE OWNER OF THE HOUSE LEADS A RECLUSIVE EXISTENCE, WITH ONLY A SINGLE SERVANT TO ATTEND TO HIM.
LITTLE IS KNOWN ABOUT THE OWNER, FOR HE IS GRUMPY AND ANTI-SOCIAL AND SHUNS CONTACT WITH THE TOWNSFOLK BELOW. RUMOR HAS IT, HOWEVER, THAT HE IS FABULOUSLY WEALTHY, AND THAT HIDDEN DEEP IN THIS HOUSE IS A TREASURE BEYOND IMAGINING.

INSIDE THE GREAT HOUSE, THE SAME ROUTINE IS OBSERVED EVERY EVENING. AFTER GORGING HIMSELF ON AN ENORMOUS MEAL OF GOURMET DELICACIES, THE OWNER RETIRES TO THE COMFORT OF HIS FAVORITE CHAIR. WITH HIS FAITHFUL DOG AT HIS FEET, HE SAVORS A FINE CIGAR AND AN AFTER-DINNER DRINK.

THE PORK CHOPS WERE SLIGHTLY OVERCOOKED, SMEDLEY. DO IT AGAIN AND YOU'RE FIRED.

VERY GOOD, SIR.

THEN COMES THE HIGHLIGHT OF HIS EVENING -- IN FACT, THE ONLY PART OF HIS ENTIRE EXISTENCE THAT GIVES HIM ANY TRUE PLEASURE -- AS HE SETTLES IN TO READ A SELECTION FROM HIS ENORMOUS LIBRARY -- A LIBRARY PAINSTAKINGLY ASSEMBLED AT UNSPEAKABLE EXPENSE THROUGH YEARS OF OBSESSIVE COLLECTING -- *THE WORLD'S GREATEST LIBRARY OF COMIC BOOKS!*

AH, *CAPTAIN SQUID* #7 -- WITH THE FIRST APPEARANCE OF HIS SIDEKICK, *LI'L SQUIDDIE!* HOW WELL I REMEMBER THE DAY I BOUGHT THIS BOOK.

"THE OWNER OF THE LOCAL COMICS SHOP REFUSED TO NEGOTIATE ON THE PRICE -- UNTIL I THREATENED TO TELL THE VICE SQUAD THAT HE WAS SELLING BETTY PAGE TRADING CARDS TO MINORS. WE SETTLED ON 10% OF GUIDE. I LEFT THE SHOP CLUTCHING MY LATEST PRIZE -- ONLY TO BE ACCOSTED BY SOME LOWLIFE LOITERING OUTSIDE."

'SCUSE ME -- DO YOU HAVE A LIGHT?

"I TAUGHT THE RUFFIAN A SHARP LESSON."

YAAAH! KEEP AWAY FROM MY PRECIOUS MINT COPY!

"OF COURSE, AFTER THAT DISTASTEFUL INCIDENT, I'LL NEVER PATRONIZE THAT STORE AGAIN."

LATER, HIS READING DONE, THE COLLECTOR COMPLETES HIS EVENING RITUAL. HE CAREFULLY RETURNS THE PRECIOUS COMIC TO ITS PROTECTIVE SLEEVE...

...THEN HE CARRIES HIS TREASURE DOWN AN ANCIENT STAIRCASE TO HIS CELLAR.

THERE, AMIDST BOXES AND CRATES OF LONG-FORGOTTEN HEIRLOOMS, HE HAS CONSTRUCTED A HOME FOR HIS COLLECTION...

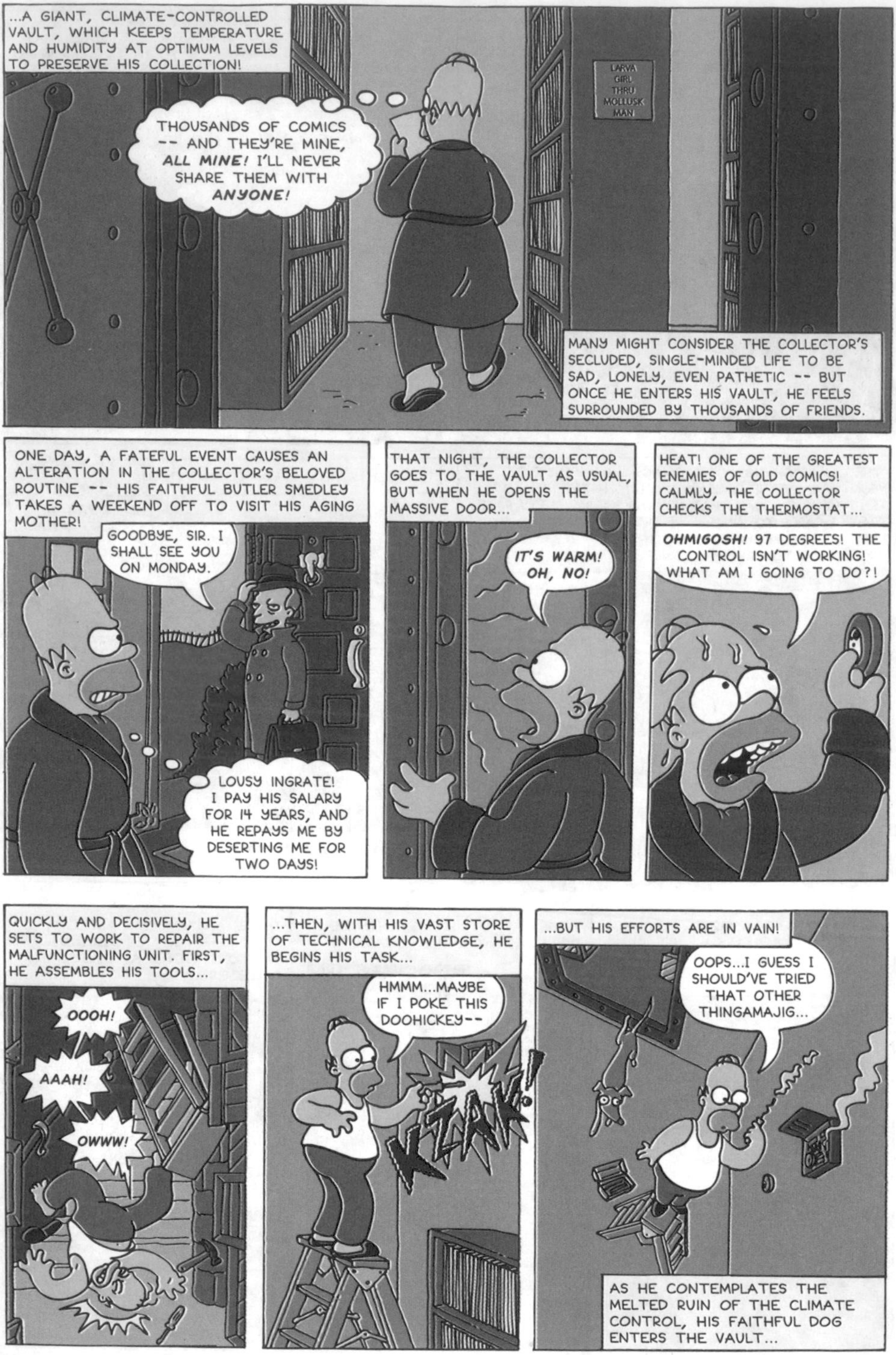
...A GIANT, CLIMATE-CONTROLLED VAULT, WHICH KEEPS TEMPERATURE AND HUMIDITY AT OPTIMUM LEVELS TO PRESERVE HIS COLLECTION!
THOUSANDS OF COMICS -- AND THEY'RE MINE, ALL MINE! I'LL NEVER SHARE THEM WITH ANYONE!
LARVA GIRL THRU MOLLUSK MAN
MANY MIGHT CONSIDER THE COLLECTOR'S SECLUDED, SINGLE-MINDED LIFE TO BE SAD, LONELY, EVEN PATHETIC -- BUT ONCE HE ENTERS HIS VAULT, HE FEELS SURROUNDED BY THOUSANDS OF FRIENDS.
ONE DAY, A FATEFUL EVENT CAUSES AN ALTERATION IN THE COLLECTOR'S BELOVED ROUTINE -- HIS FAITHFUL BUTLER SMEDLEY TAKES A WEEKEND OFF TO VISIT HIS AGING MOTHER!
GOODBYE, SIR. I SHALL SEE YOU ON MONDAY.
LOUSY INGRATE! I PAY HIS SALARY FOR 14 YEARS, AND HE REPAYS ME BY DESERTING ME FOR TWO DAYS!
THAT NIGHT, THE COLLECTOR GOES TO THE VAULT AS USUAL, BUT WHEN HE OPENS THE MASSIVE DOOR...
IT'S WARM! OH, NO!
HEAT! ONE OF THE GREATEST ENEMIES OF OLD COMICS! CALMLY, THE COLLECTOR CHECKS THE THERMOSTAT...
OHMIGOSH! 97 DEGREES! THE CONTROL ISN'T WORKING! WHAT AM I GOING TO DO?!
QUICKLY AND DECISIVELY, HE SETS TO WORK TO REPAIR THE MALFUNCTIONING UNIT. FIRST, HE ASSEMBLES HIS TOOLS...
OOOH!
AAAH!
OWWW!
...THEN, WITH HIS VAST STORE OF TECHNICAL KNOWLEDGE, HE BEGINS HIS TASK...
HMMM...MAYBE IF I POKE THIS DOOHICKEY--
KZAK!
...BUT HIS EFFORTS ARE IN VAIN!
OOPS...I GUESS I SHOULD'VE TRIED THAT OTHER THINGAMAJIG...
AS HE CONTEMPLATES THE MELTED RUIN OF THE CLIMATE CONTROL, HIS FAITHFUL DOG ENTERS THE VAULT...

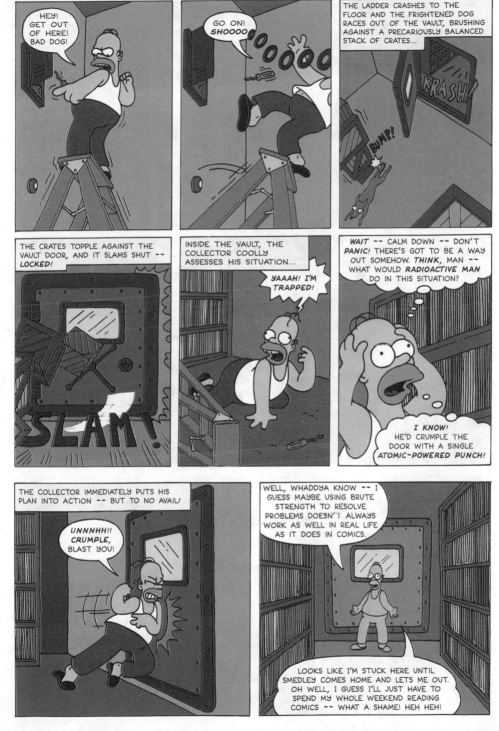

37

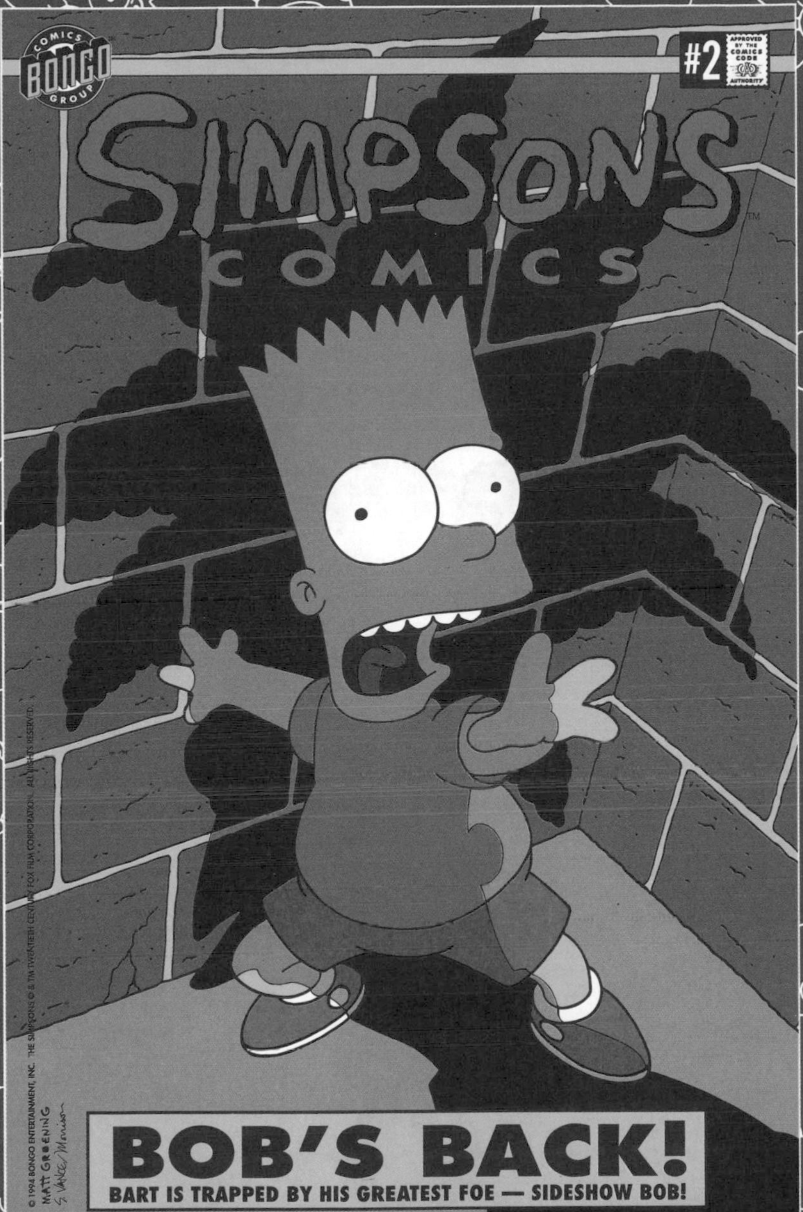
BONGO COMICS GROUP
#2
APPROVED BY THE COMICS CODE AUTHORITY
SIMPSONS COMICS
BOB'S BACK!
BART IS TRAPPED BY HIS GREATEST FOE — SIDESHOW BOB!
© 1994 BONGO ENTERTAINMENT, INC. THE SIMPSONS © & TM TWENTIETH CENTURY FOX FILM CORPORATION. ALL RIGHTS RESERVED.
MATT GROENING

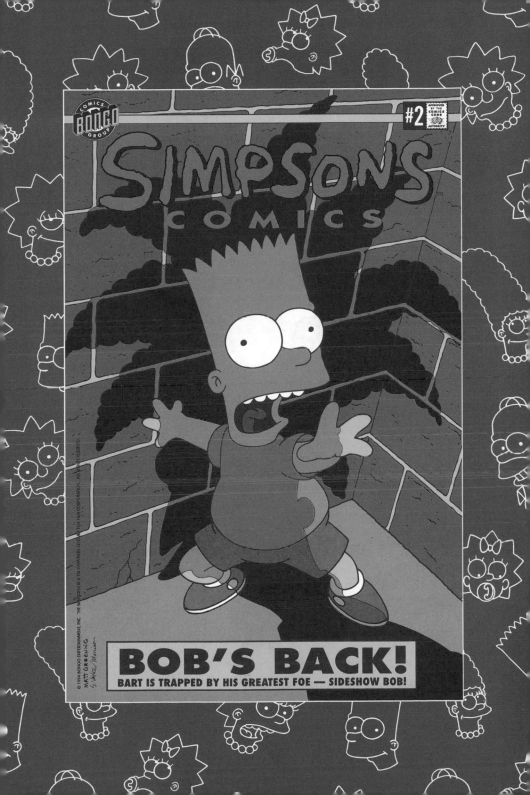

BECAUSE YOU DEMANDED IT, BONGO PRESENTS...

Patty & Selma's FASCINATIN' FASHIONS!

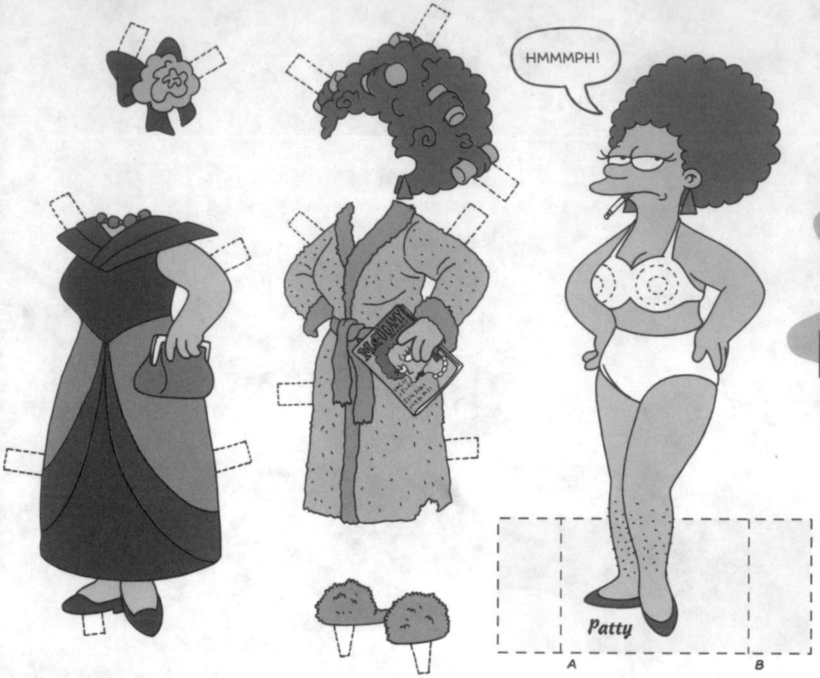
HMMMPH!
Patty
A
B

CUT OUT FIGURES (OR BETTER YET, USE A PHOTOCOPY!) AND PASTE ON LIGHTWEIGHT CARDBOARD. TO STAND, FOLD BASE AT *A* AND *B*.

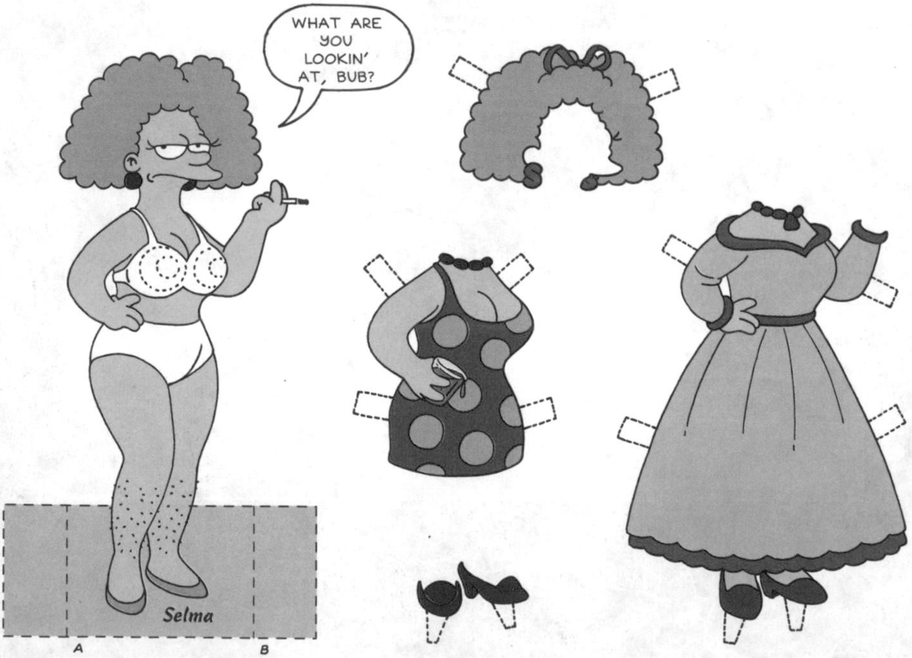
WHAT ARE YOU LOOKIN' AT, BUB?
Selma
A
B

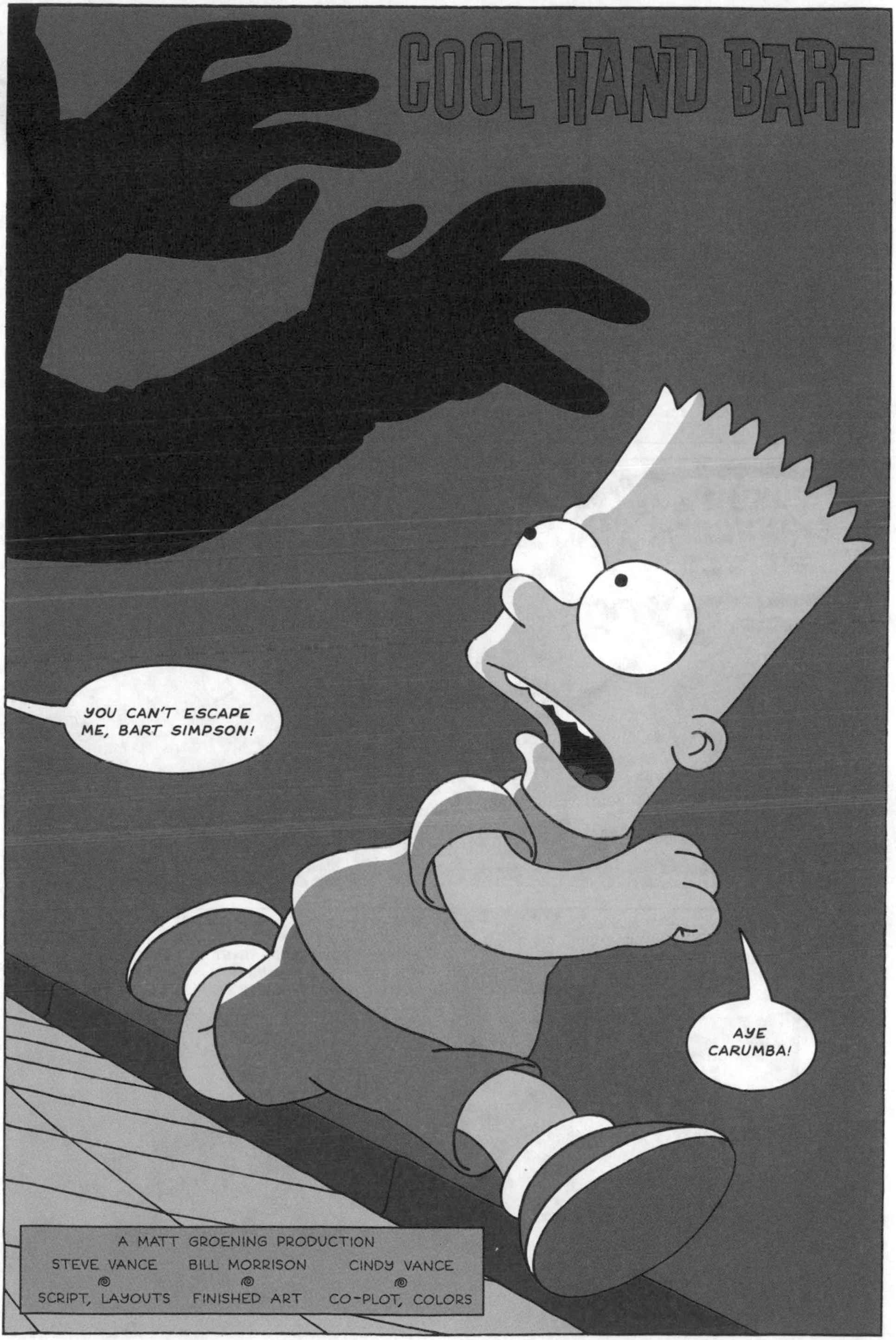
COOL HAND BART
YOU CAN'T ESCAPE ME, BART SIMPSON!
AYE CARUMBA!
A MATT GROENING PRODUCTION
STEVE VANCE SCRIPT, LAYOUTS
BILL MORRISON FINISHED ART
CINDY VANCE CO-PLOT, COLORS

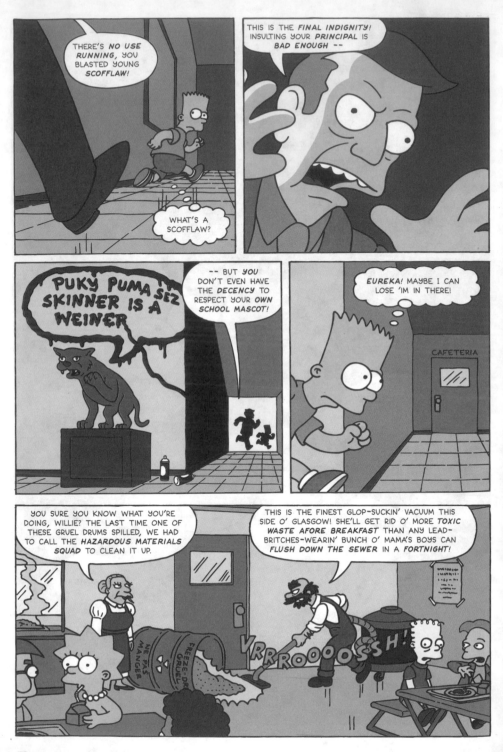

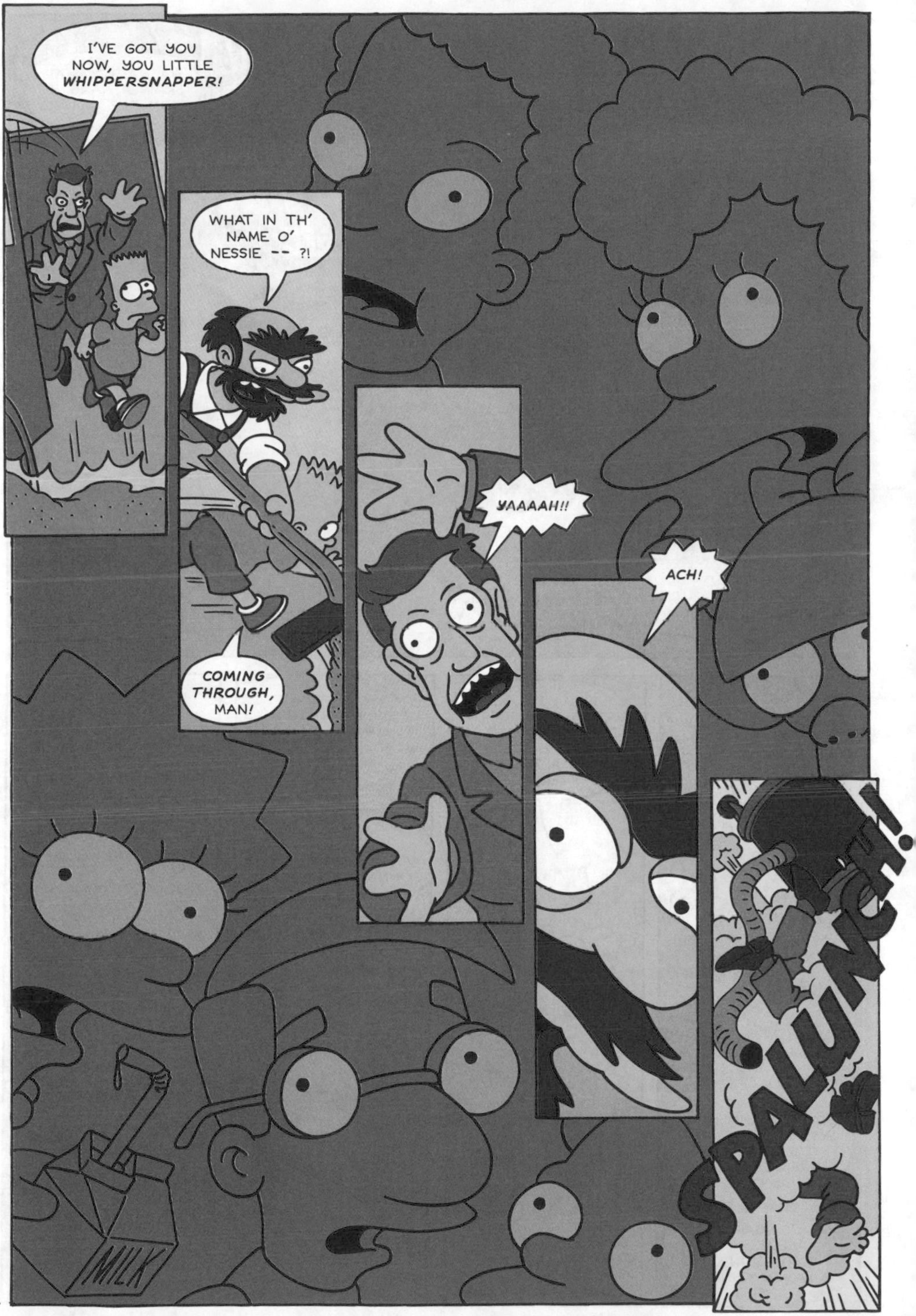

I'VE GOT YOU NOW, YOU LITTLE WHIPPERSNAPPER!
WHAT IN TH' NAME O' NESSIE -- ?!
COMING THROUGH, MAN!
YAAAAH!!
ACH!
SPALUNCH!
MILK

44

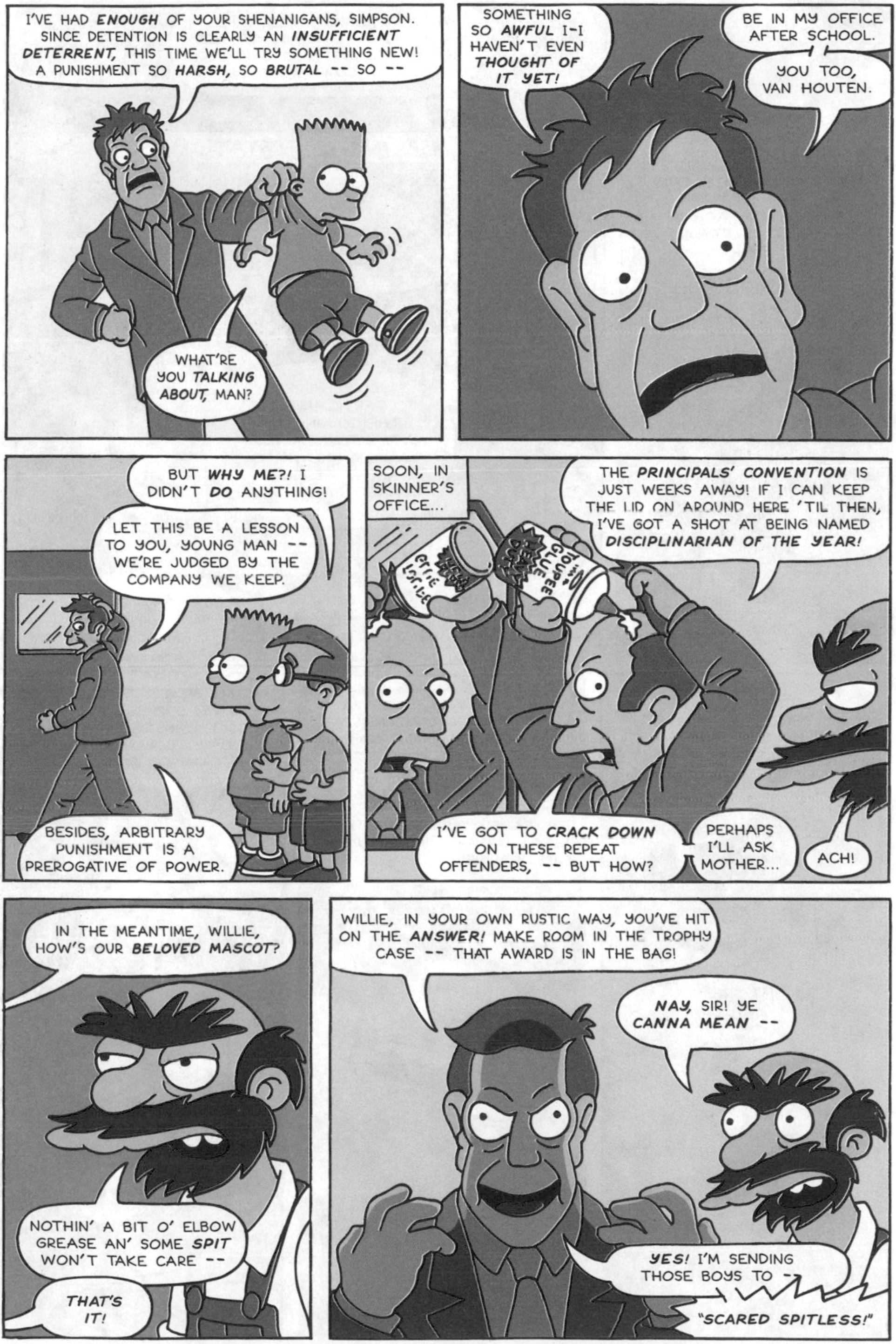

I'VE HAD ENOUGH OF YOUR SHENANIGANS, SIMPSON. SINCE DETENTION IS CLEARLY AN INSUFFICIENT DETERRENT, THIS TIME WE'LL TRY SOMETHING NEW! A PUNISHMENT SO HARSH, SO BRUTAL -- SO --
WHAT'RE YOU TALKING ABOUT, MAN?
SOMETHING SO AWFUL I-I HAVEN'T EVEN THOUGHT OF IT YET!
BE IN MY OFFICE AFTER SCHOOL.
YOU TOO, VAN HOUTEN.
BUT WHY ME?! I DIDN'T DO ANYTHING!
LET THIS BE A LESSON TO YOU, YOUNG MAN -- WE'RE JUDGED BY THE COMPANY WE KEEP.
BESIDES, ARBITRARY PUNISHMENT IS A PREROGATIVE OF POWER.
SOON, IN SKINNER'S OFFICE...
THE PRINCIPALS' CONVENTION IS JUST WEEKS AWAY! IF I CAN KEEP THE LID ON AROUND HERE 'TIL THEN, I'VE GOT A SHOT AT BEING NAMED DISCIPLINARIAN OF THE YEAR!
TOUPEE GLUE
I'VE GOT TO CRACK DOWN ON THESE REPEAT OFFENDERS, -- BUT HOW?
PERHAPS I'LL ASK MOTHER...
ACH!
IN THE MEANTIME, WILLIE, HOW'S OUR BELOVED MASCOT?
NOTHIN' A BIT O' ELBOW GREASE AN' SOME SPIT WON'T TAKE CARE --
THAT'S IT!
WILLIE, IN YOUR OWN RUSTIC WAY, YOU'VE HIT ON THE ANSWER! MAKE ROOM IN THE TROPHY CASE -- THAT AWARD IS IN THE BAG!
NAY, SIR! YE CANNA MEAN --
YES! I'M SENDING THOSE BOYS TO --
"SCARED SPITLESS!"

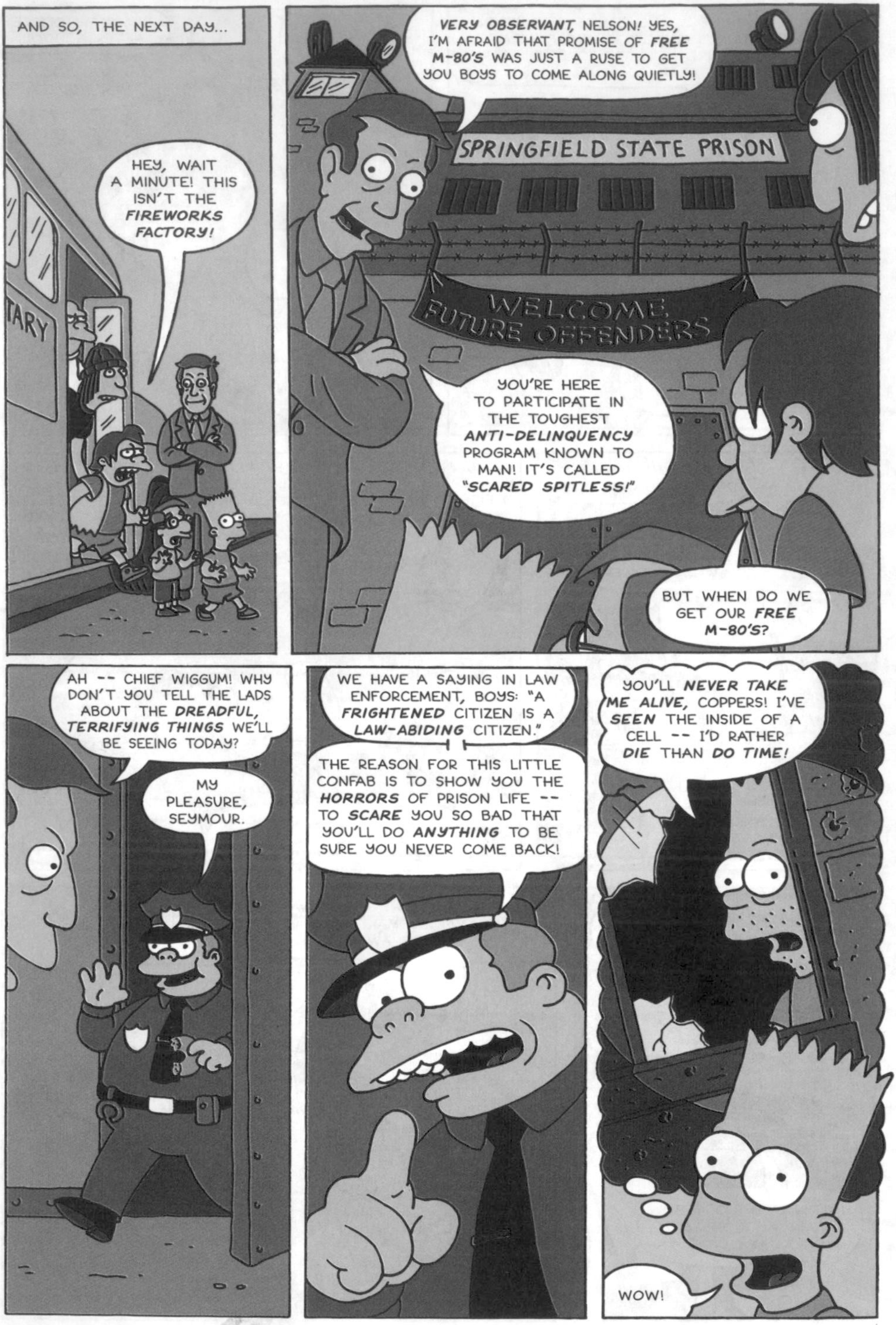
AND SO, THE NEXT DAY...
HEY, WAIT A MINUTE! THIS ISN'T THE FIREWORKS FACTORY!
TARY
VERY OBSERVANT, NELSON! YES, I'M AFRAID THAT PROMISE OF FREE M-80'S WAS JUST A RUSE TO GET YOU BOYS TO COME ALONG QUIETLY!
SPRINGFIELD STATE PRISON
WELCOME FUTURE OFFENDERS
YOU'RE HERE TO PARTICIPATE IN THE TOUGHEST ANTI-DELINQUENCY PROGRAM KNOWN TO MAN! IT'S CALLED "SCARED SPITLESS!"
BUT WHEN DO WE GET OUR FREE M-80'S?
AH -- CHIEF WIGGUM! WHY DON'T YOU TELL THE LADS ABOUT THE DREADFUL, TERRIFYING THINGS WE'LL BE SEEING TODAY?
MY PLEASURE, SEYMOUR.
WE HAVE A SAYING IN LAW ENFORCEMENT, BOYS: "A FRIGHTENED CITIZEN IS A LAW-ABIDING CITIZEN."
THE REASON FOR THIS LITTLE CONFAB IS TO SHOW YOU THE HORRORS OF PRISON LIFE -- TO SCARE YOU SO BAD THAT YOU'LL DO ANYTHING TO BE SURE YOU NEVER COME BACK!
YOU'LL NEVER TAKE ME ALIVE, COPPERS! I'VE SEEN THE INSIDE OF A CELL -- I'D RATHER DIE THAN DO TIME!
WOW!

47

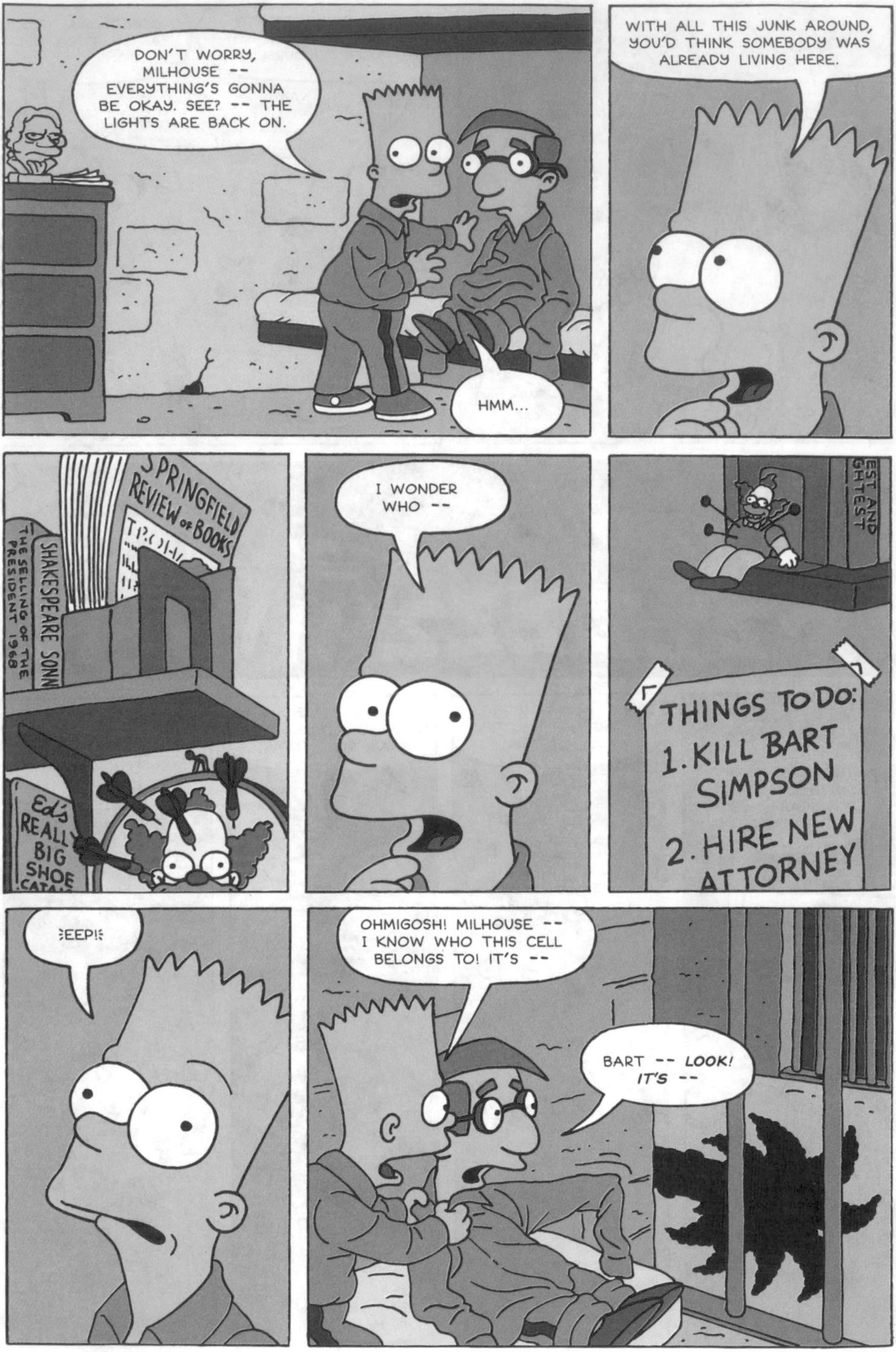
DON'T WORRY, MILHOUSE -- EVERYTHING'S GONNA BE OKAY. SEE? -- THE LIGHTS ARE BACK ON.
HMM...
WITH ALL THIS JUNK AROUND, YOU'D THINK SOMEBODY WAS ALREADY LIVING HERE.
SPRINGFIELD REVIEW OF BOOKS
THE SELLING OF THE PRESIDENT 1968
I WONDER WHO --
THINGS TO DO:
1. KILL BART SIMPSON
2. HIRE NEW ATTORNEY
EEP!
OHMIGOSH! MILHOUSE -- I KNOW WHO THIS CELL BELONGS TO! IT'S --
BART -- LOOK! IT'S --

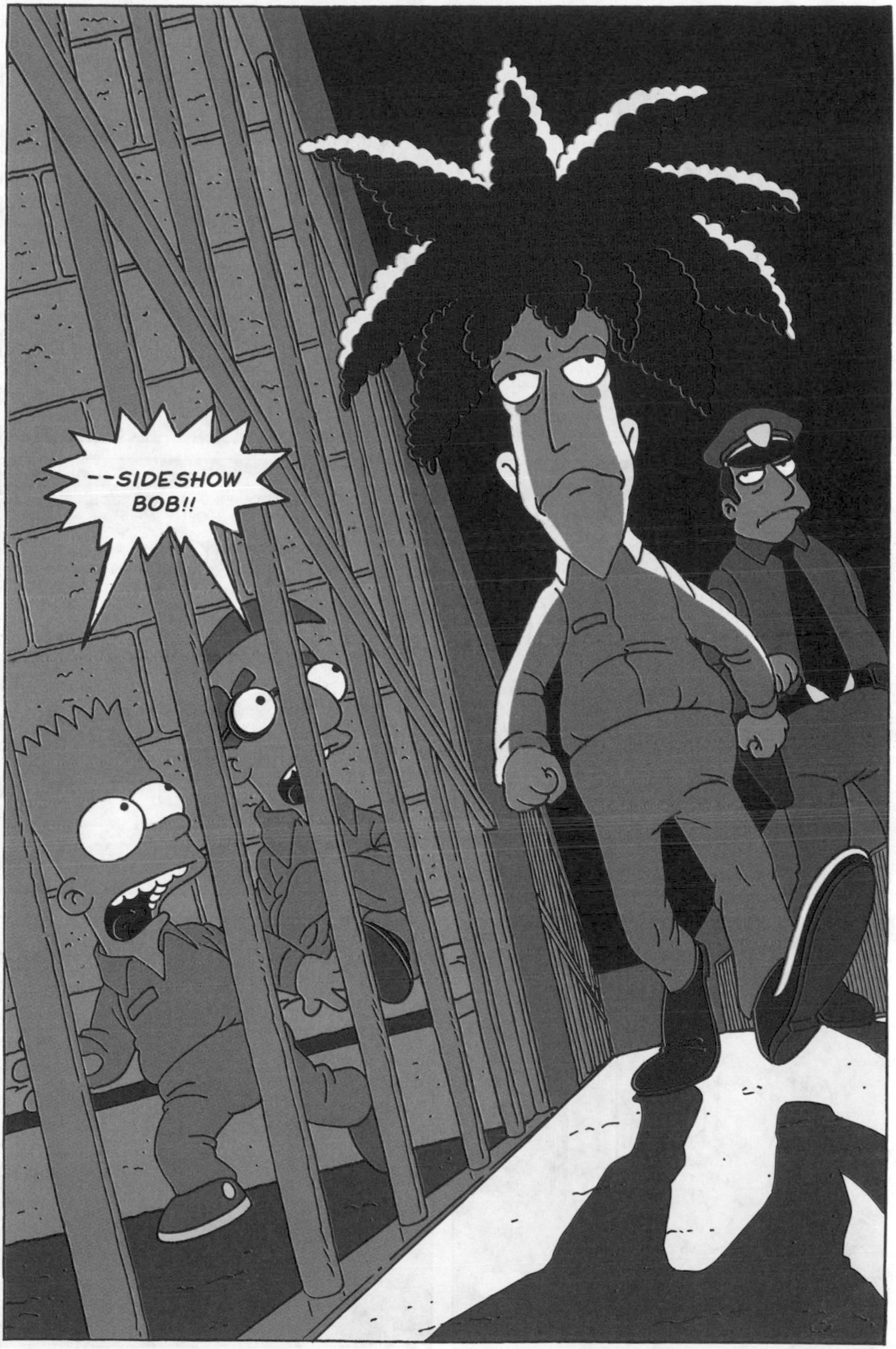
--SIDESHOW BOB!!

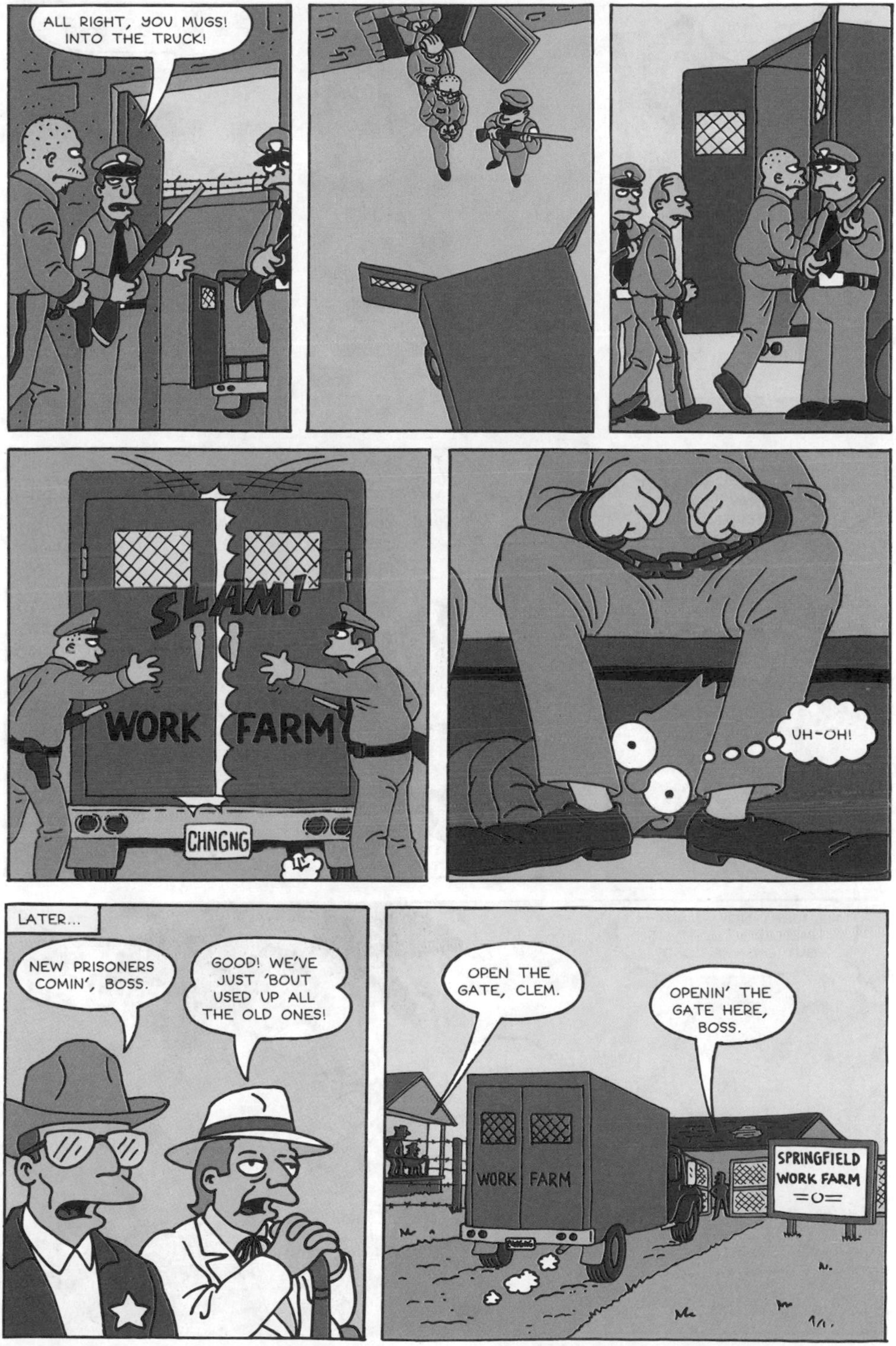
ALL RIGHT, YOU MUGS! INTO THE TRUCK!
SLAM!
WORK FARM
CHNGNG
UH-OH!
LATER...
NEW PRISONERS COMIN', BOSS.
GOOD! WE'VE JUST 'BOUT USED UP ALL THE OLD ONES!
OPEN THE GATE, CLEM.
OPENIN' THE GATE HERE, BOSS.
WORK FARM
SPRINGFIELD WORK FARM

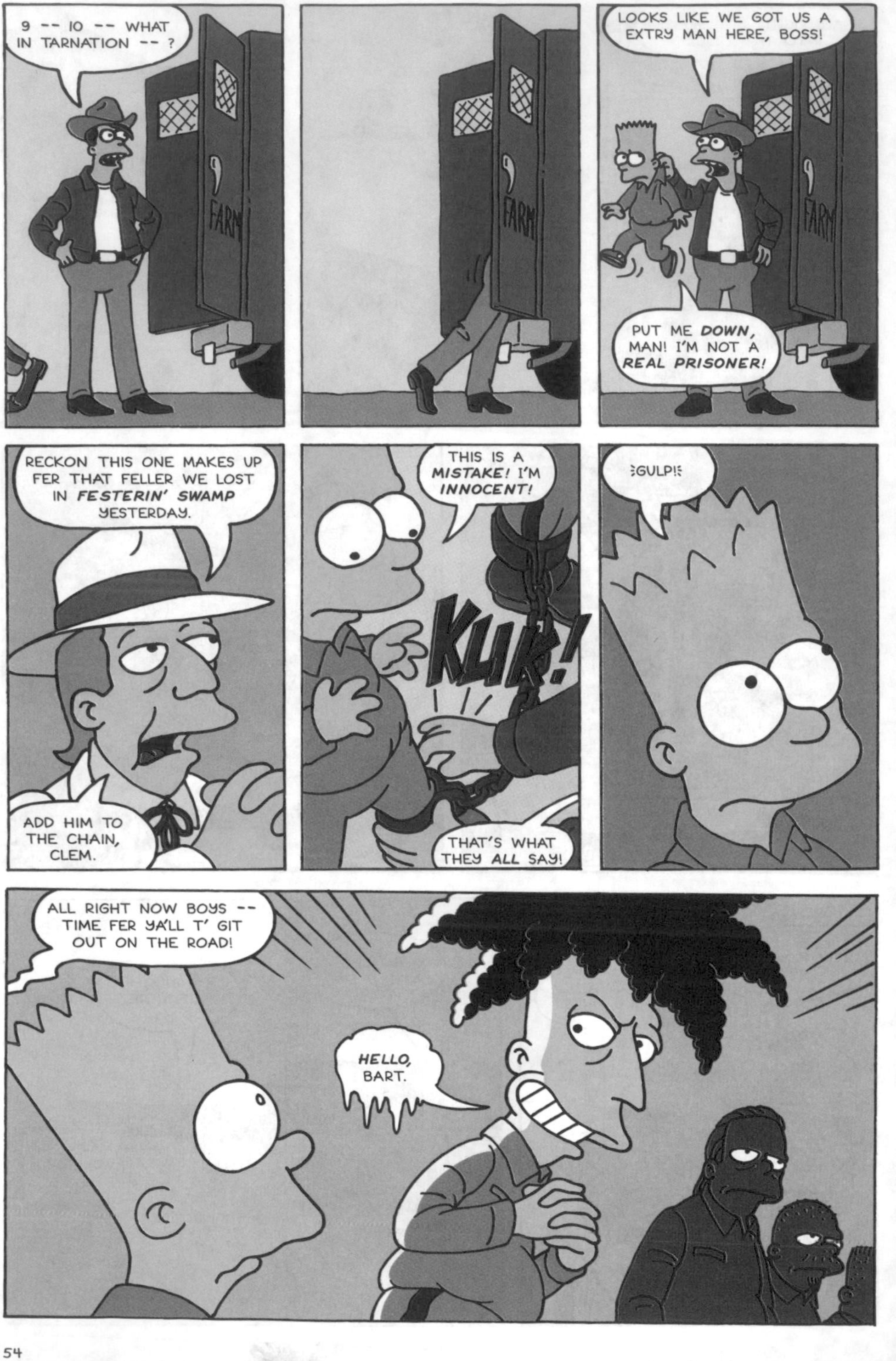
9 -- 10 -- WHAT IN TARNATION -- ?
LOOKS LIKE WE GOT US A EXTRY MAN HERE, BOSS!
PUT ME DOWN, MAN! I'M NOT A REAL PRISONER!
RECKON THIS ONE MAKES UP FER THAT FELLER WE LOST IN FESTERIN' SWAMP YESTERDAY.
ADD HIM TO THE CHAIN, CLEM.
THIS IS A MISTAKE! I'M INNOCENT!
KUK!
THAT'S WHAT THEY ALL SAY!
GULP!
ALL RIGHT NOW BOYS -- TIME FER YA'LL T' GIT OUT ON THE ROAD!
HELLO, BART.

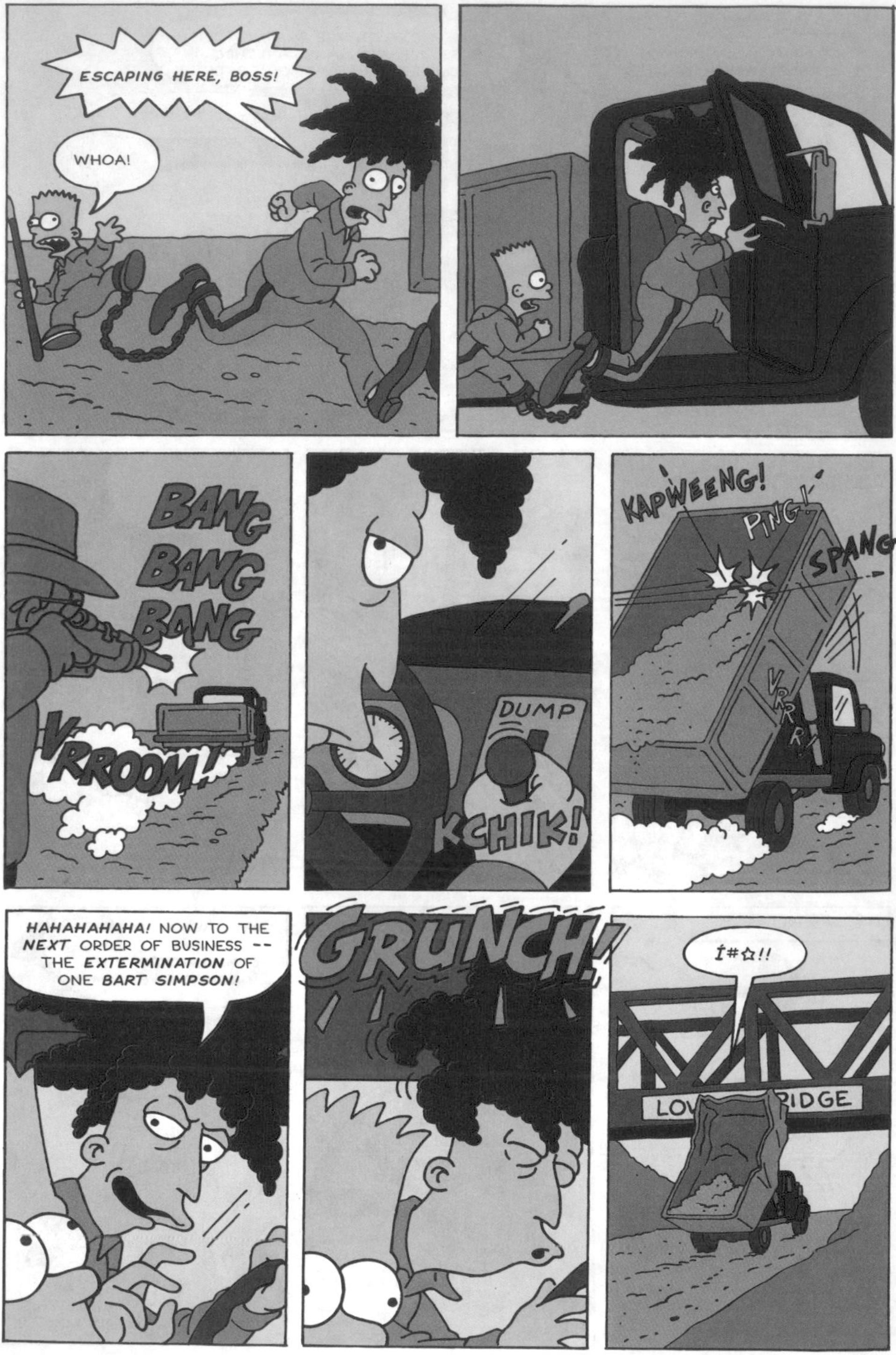

ESCAPING HERE, BOSS!
WHOA!
BANG
BANG
BANG
VRROOM!
DUMP
KCHIK!
KAPWEENG!
PING!
SPANG!
VRRR!
HAHAHAHAHA! NOW TO THE NEXT ORDER OF BUSINESS -- THE EXTERMINATION OF ONE BART SIMPSON!
GRUNCH!
LOV RIDGE

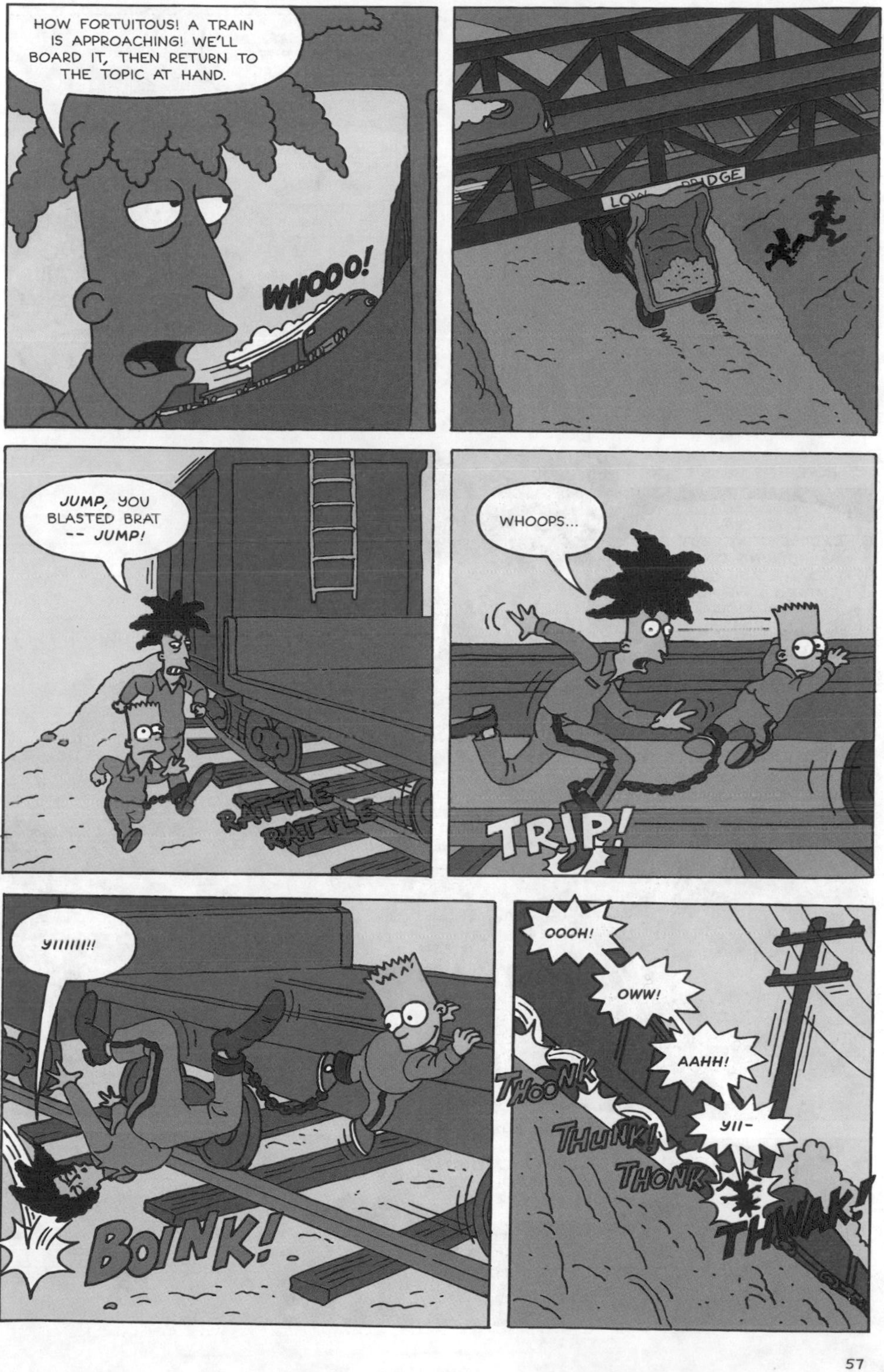
HOW FORTUITOUS! A TRAIN IS APPROACHING! WE'LL BOARD IT, THEN RETURN TO THE TOPIC AT HAND.
WHOOO!
JUMP, YOU BLASTED BRAT -- JUMP!
RATTLE
RATTLE
WHOOPS...
TRIP!
YIIIIII!!
BOINK!
OOOH!
OWW!
AAHH!
YII-
THOONK
THUNK!
THONK
THWAK!

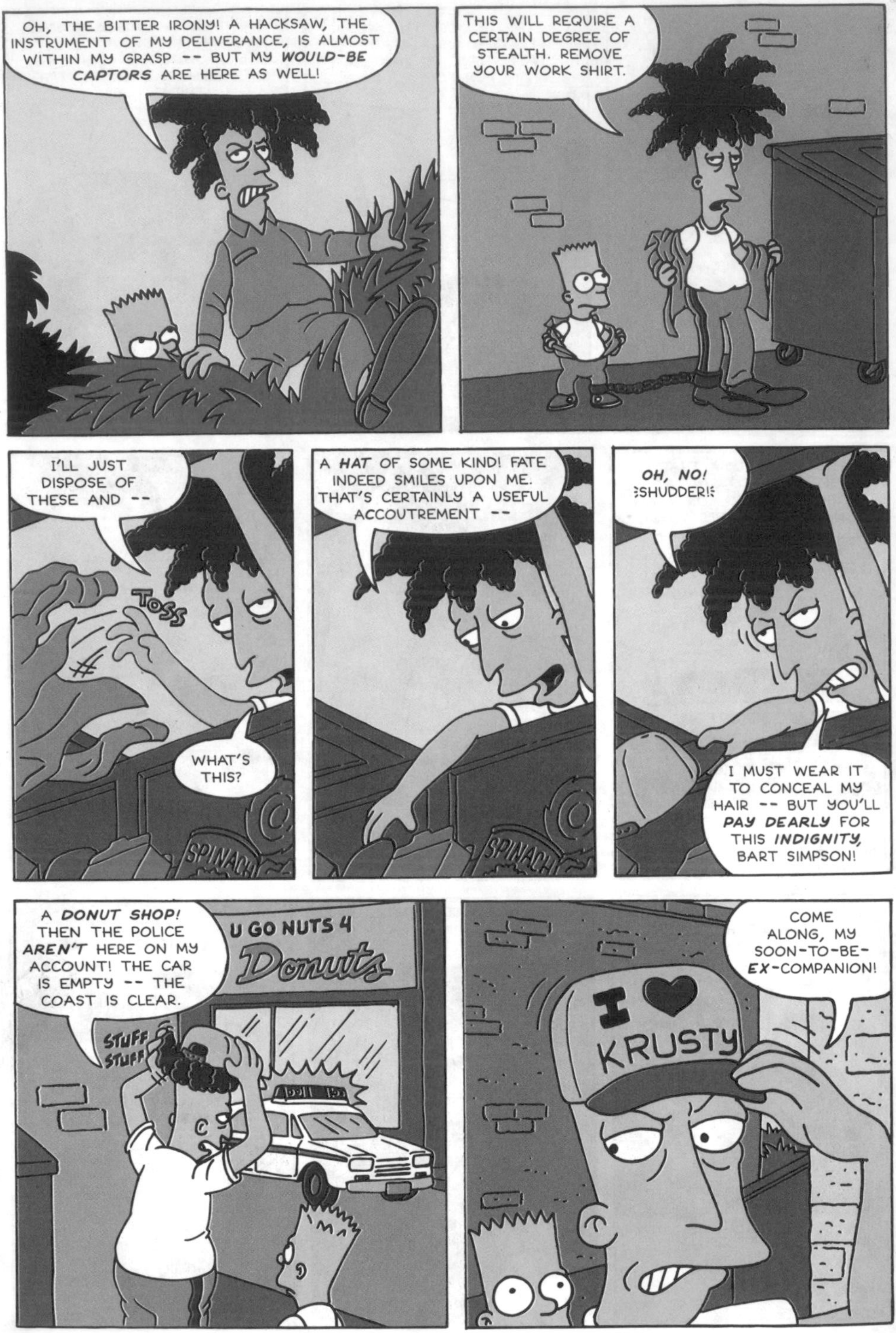
OH, THE BITTER IRONY! A HACKSAW, THE INSTRUMENT OF MY DELIVERANCE, IS ALMOST WITHIN MY GRASP -- BUT MY ***WOULD-BE CAPTORS*** ARE HERE AS WELL!
THIS WILL REQUIRE A CERTAIN DEGREE OF STEALTH. REMOVE YOUR WORK SHIRT.
I'LL JUST DISPOSE OF THESE AND --
TOSS
WHAT'S THIS?
A ***HAT*** OF SOME KIND! FATE INDEED SMILES UPON ME. THAT'S CERTAINLY A USEFUL ACCOUTREMENT --
SPINACH
OH, NO!
:SHUDDER!:
I MUST WEAR IT TO CONCEAL MY HAIR -- BUT YOU'LL ***PAY DEARLY*** FOR THIS ***INDIGNITY,*** BART SIMPSON!
A ***DONUT SHOP!*** THEN THE POLICE ***AREN'T*** HERE ON MY ACCOUNT! THE CAR IS EMPTY -- THE COAST IS CLEAR.
U GO NUTS 4
Donuts
STUFF
STUFF
COME ALONG, MY SOON-TO-BE-***EX***-COMPANION!
I ♥ KRUSTY

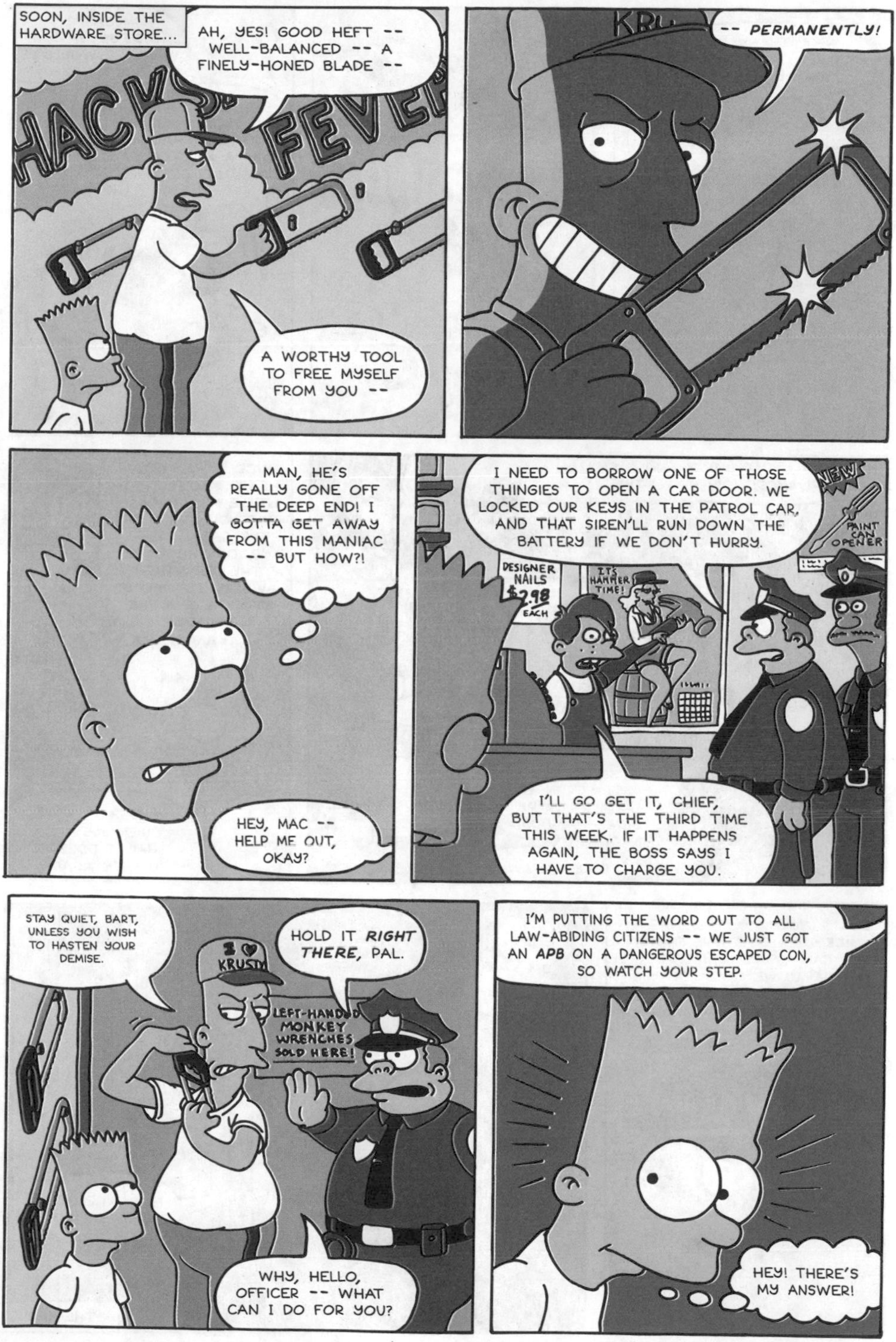

SOON, INSIDE THE HARDWARE STORE...
AH, YES! GOOD HEFT -- WELL-BALANCED -- A FINELY-HONED BLADE --
HACKSAW FEVER
A WORTHY TOOL TO FREE MYSELF FROM YOU --
-- PERMANENTLY!
MAN, HE'S REALLY GONE OFF THE DEEP END! I GOTTA GET AWAY FROM THIS MANIAC -- BUT HOW?!
HEY, MAC -- HELP ME OUT, OKAY?
I NEED TO BORROW ONE OF THOSE THINGIES TO OPEN A CAR DOOR. WE LOCKED OUR KEYS IN THE PATROL CAR, AND THAT SIREN'LL RUN DOWN THE BATTERY IF WE DON'T HURRY.
NEW
PAINT CAN OPENER
DESIGNER NAILS $2.98 EACH
IT'S HAMMER TIME!
I'LL GO GET IT, CHIEF, BUT THAT'S THE THIRD TIME THIS WEEK. IF IT HAPPENS AGAIN, THE BOSS SAYS I HAVE TO CHARGE YOU.
STAY QUIET, BART, UNLESS YOU WISH TO HASTEN YOUR DEMISE.
HOLD IT *RIGHT THERE,* PAL.
I ♥ KRUSTY
LEFT-HANDED MONKEY WRENCHES SOLD HERE!
WHY, HELLO, OFFICER -- WHAT CAN I DO FOR YOU?
I'M PUTTING THE WORD OUT TO ALL LAW-ABIDING CITIZENS -- WE JUST GOT AN *APB* ON A DANGEROUS ESCAPED CON, SO WATCH YOUR STEP.
HEY! THERE'S MY ANSWER!

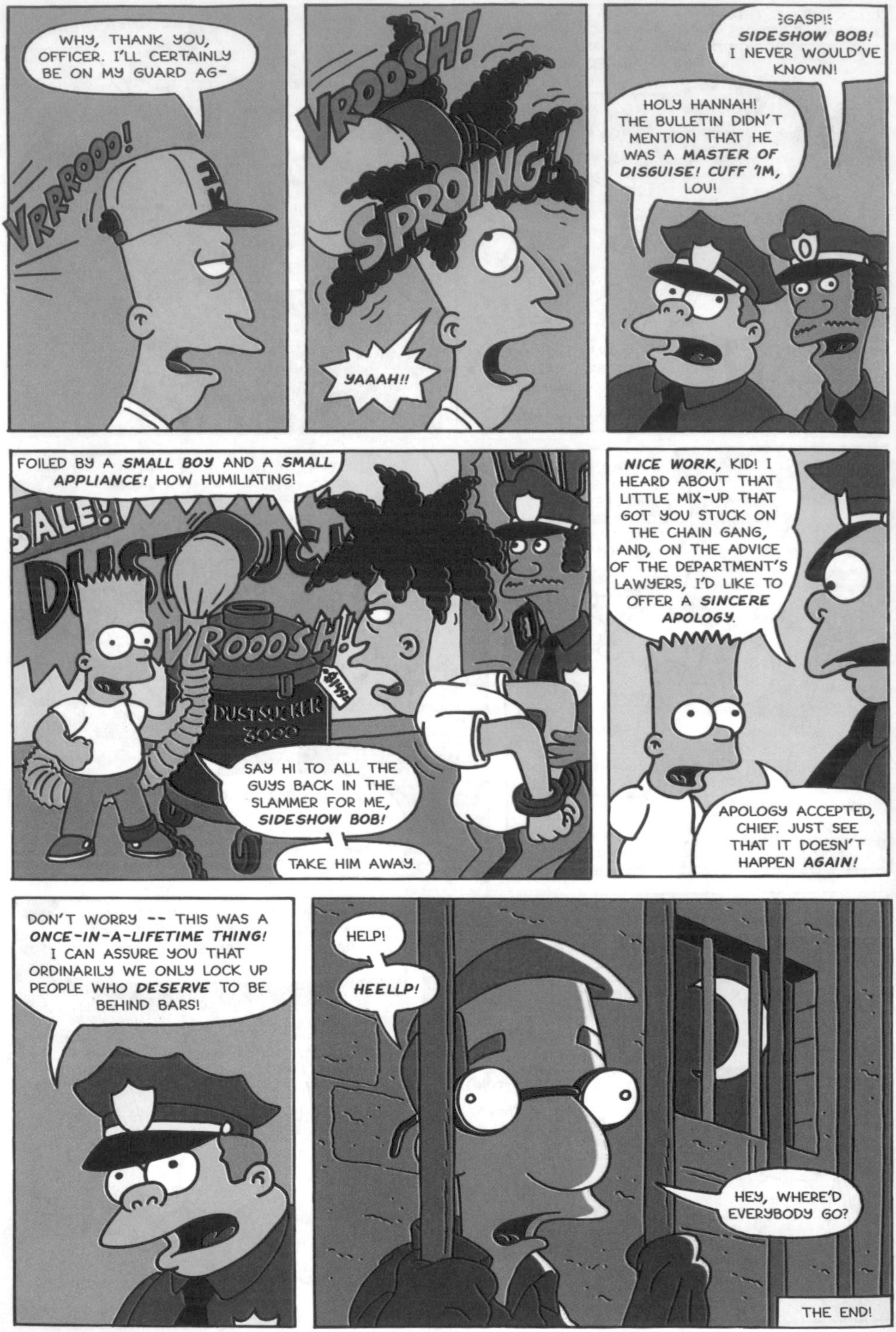
WHY, THANK YOU, OFFICER. I'LL CERTAINLY BE ON MY GUARD AG-
VRRROOO!
VROOSH!
SPROING!
YAAAH!!
GASP! SIDESHOW BOB! I NEVER WOULD'VE KNOWN!
HOLY HANNAH! THE BULLETIN DIDN'T MENTION THAT HE WAS A MASTER OF DISGUISE! CUFF 'IM, LOU!
FOILED BY A SMALL BOY AND A SMALL APPLIANCE! HOW HUMILIATING!
SALE!
VROOOSH!
DUSTSUCKER 3000
SAY HI TO ALL THE GUYS BACK IN THE SLAMMER FOR ME, SIDESHOW BOB!
TAKE HIM AWAY.
NICE WORK, KID! I HEARD ABOUT THAT LITTLE MIX-UP THAT GOT YOU STUCK ON THE CHAIN GANG, AND, ON THE ADVICE OF THE DEPARTMENT'S LAWYERS, I'D LIKE TO OFFER A SINCERE APOLOGY.
APOLOGY ACCEPTED, CHIEF. JUST SEE THAT IT DOESN'T HAPPEN AGAIN!
DON'T WORRY -- THIS WAS A ONCE-IN-A-LIFETIME THING! I CAN ASSURE YOU THAT ORDINARILY WE ONLY LOCK UP PEOPLE WHO DESERVE TO BE BEHIND BARS!
HELP!
HEELLP!
HEY, WHERE'D EVERYBODY GO?
THE END!

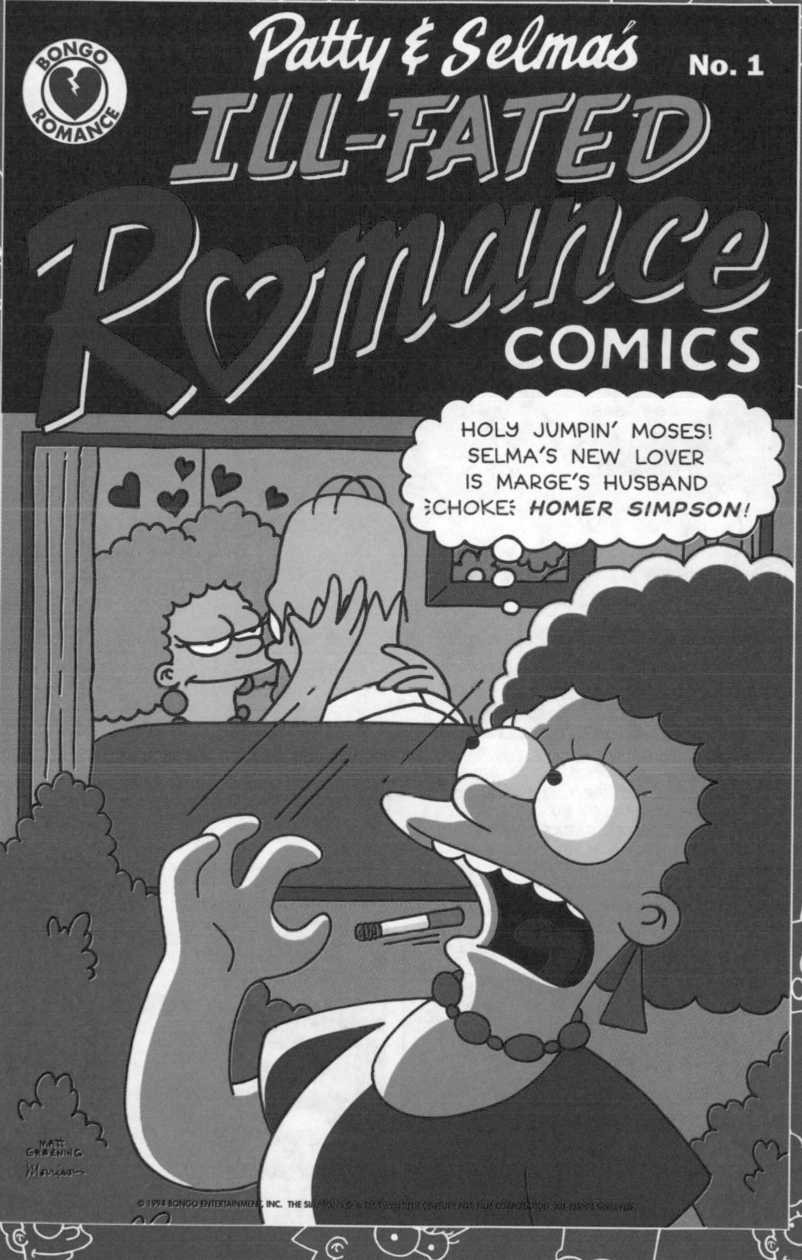
Patty & Selma's
No. 1
BONGO ROMANCE
ILL-FATED
Romance
COMICS
HOLY JUMPIN' MOSES! SELMA'S NEW LOVER IS MARGE'S HUSBAND :CHOKE: HOMER SIMPSON!
MATT GROENING
© 1994 BONGO ENTERTAINMENT, INC.

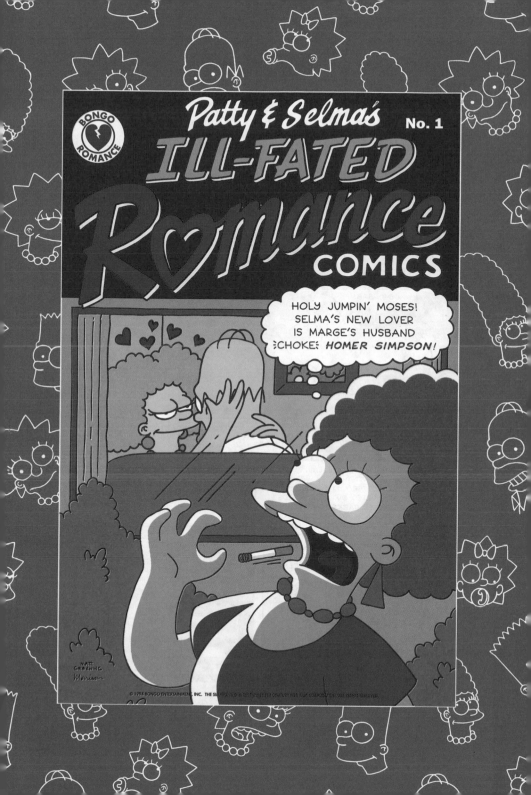

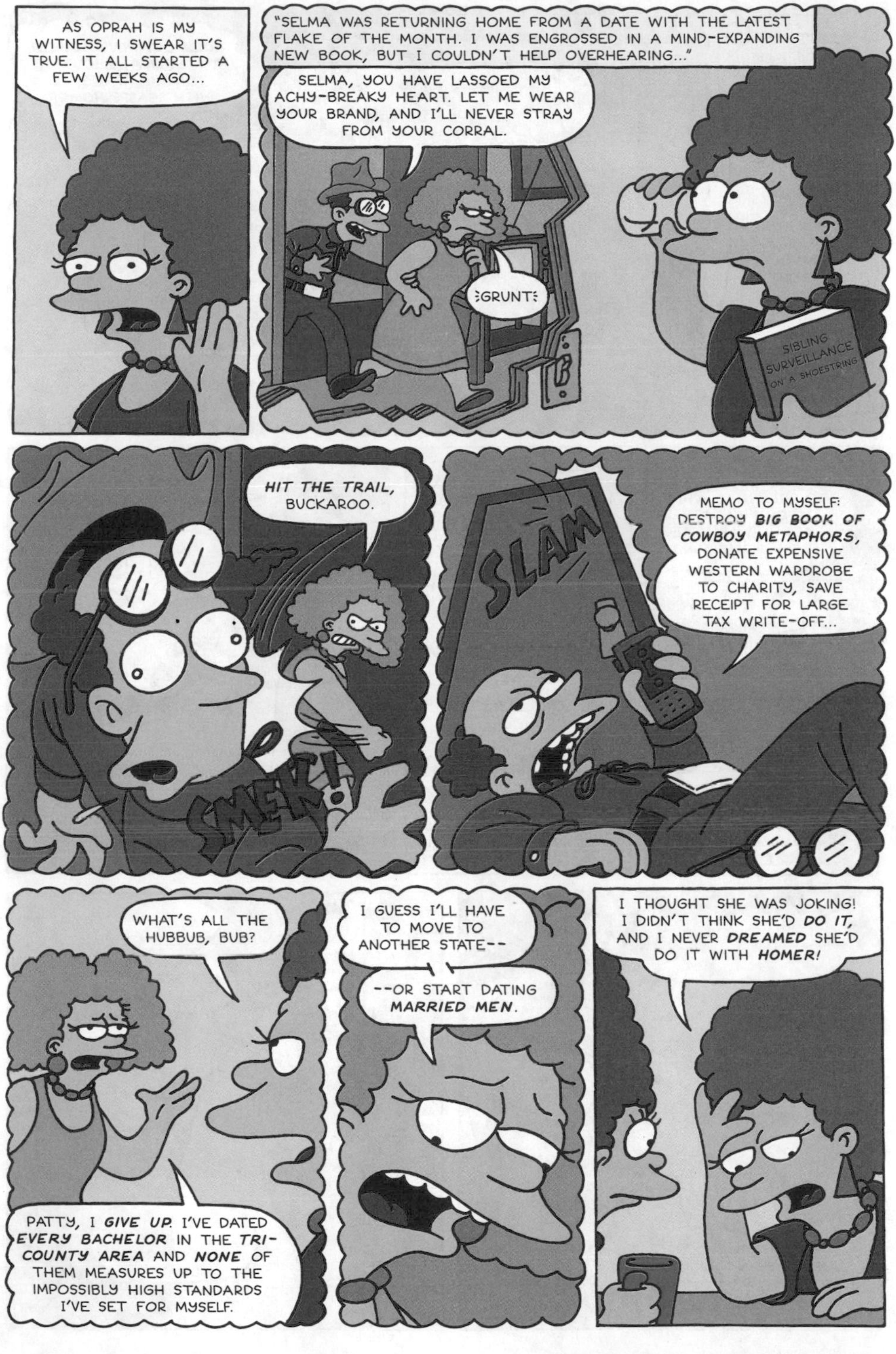

AS OPRAH IS MY WITNESS, I SWEAR IT'S TRUE. IT ALL STARTED A FEW WEEKS AGO...
"SELMA WAS RETURNING HOME FROM A DATE WITH THE LATEST FLAKE OF THE MONTH. I WAS ENGROSSED IN A MIND-EXPANDING NEW BOOK, BUT I COULDN'T HELP OVERHEARING..."
SELMA, YOU HAVE LASSOED MY ACHY-BREAKY HEART. LET ME WEAR YOUR BRAND, AND I'LL NEVER STRAY FROM YOUR CORRAL.
GRUNT
SIBLING SURVEILLANCE ON A SHOESTRING
HIT THE TRAIL, BUCKAROO.
SMEK!
SLAM
MEMO TO MYSELF: DESTROY BIG BOOK OF COWBOY METAPHORS, DONATE EXPENSIVE WESTERN WARDROBE TO CHARITY, SAVE RECEIPT FOR LARGE TAX WRITE-OFF...
WHAT'S ALL THE HUBBUB, BUB?
PATTY, I GIVE UP. I'VE DATED EVERY BACHELOR IN THE TRI-COUNTY AREA AND NONE OF THEM MEASURES UP TO THE IMPOSSIBLY HIGH STANDARDS I'VE SET FOR MYSELF.
I GUESS I'LL HAVE TO MOVE TO ANOTHER STATE--
--OR START DATING MARRIED MEN.
I THOUGHT SHE WAS JOKING! I DIDN'T THINK SHE'D DO IT, AND I NEVER DREAMED SHE'D DO IT WITH HOMER!

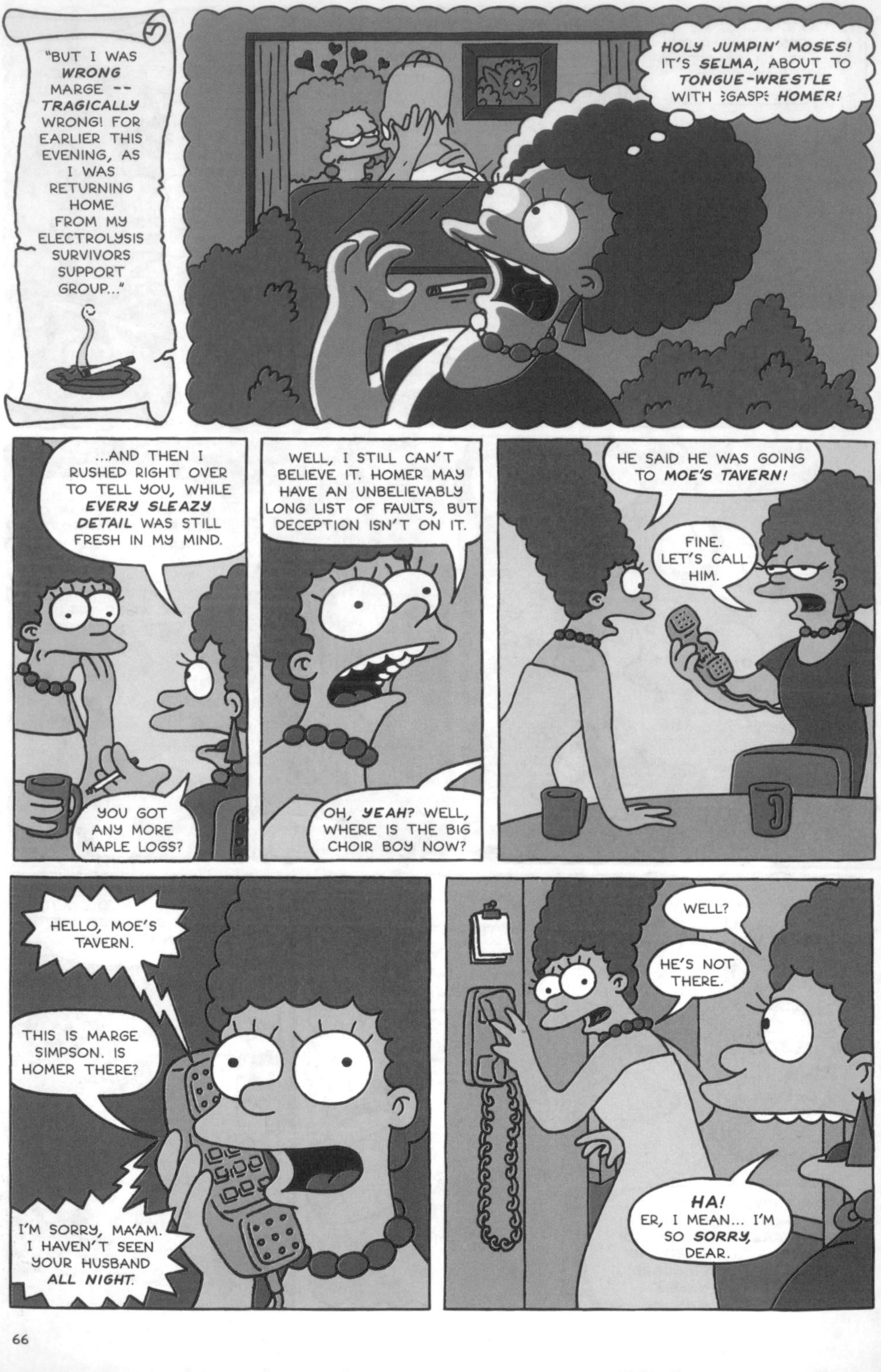
"BUT I WAS WRONG MARGE -- TRAGICALLY WRONG! FOR EARLIER THIS EVENING, AS I WAS RETURNING HOME FROM MY ELECTROLYSIS SURVIVORS SUPPORT GROUP..."
HOLY JUMPIN' MOSES! IT'S SELMA, ABOUT TO TONGUE-WRESTLE WITH ⁝GASP⁝ HOMER!
...AND THEN I RUSHED RIGHT OVER TO TELL YOU, WHILE EVERY SLEAZY DETAIL WAS STILL FRESH IN MY MIND.
YOU GOT ANY MORE MAPLE LOGS?
WELL, I STILL CAN'T BELIEVE IT. HOMER MAY HAVE AN UNBELIEVABLY LONG LIST OF FAULTS, BUT DECEPTION ISN'T ON IT.
OH, YEAH? WELL, WHERE IS THE BIG CHOIR BOY NOW?
HE SAID HE WAS GOING TO MOE'S TAVERN!
FINE. LET'S CALL HIM.
HELLO, MOE'S TAVERN.
THIS IS MARGE SIMPSON. IS HOMER THERE?
I'M SORRY, MA'AM. I HAVEN'T SEEN YOUR HUSBAND ALL NIGHT.
WELL?
HE'S NOT THERE.
HA! ER, I MEAN... I'M SO SORRY, DEAR.

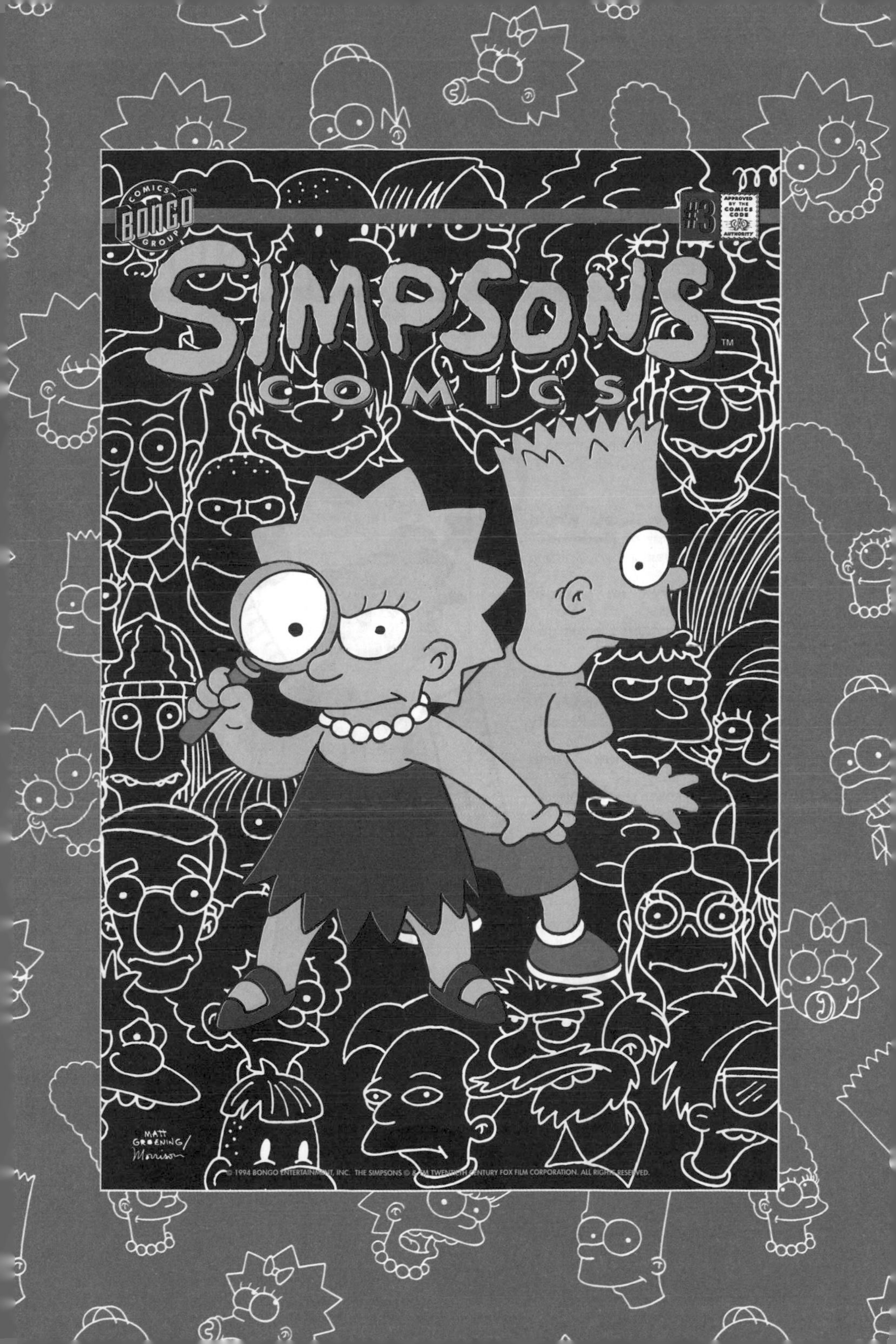
COMICS BONGO GROUP
#3
APPROVED BY THE COMICS CODE AUTHORITY
SIMPSONS COMICS
MATT GROENING/ Morrison
© 1994 BONGO ENTERTAINMENT, INC. THE SIMPSONS © & TM TWENTIETH CENTURY FOX FILM CORPORATION. ALL RIGHTS RESERVED.

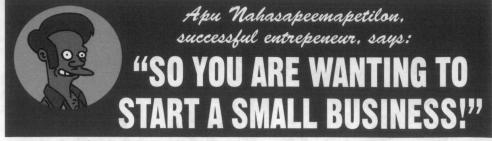

Apu Nahasapeemapetilon, successful entrepeneur, says:

"SO YOU ARE WANTING TO START A SMALL BUSINESS!"

Congratulations, my friend, on taking your first step on the road to opportunity! Now I, as proprietor of one of Springfield's most successful convenience-oriented retail establishments, am offering to you many helpful clues for the purpose of beginning an enterprise you may call your own.

Now available for the first time anywhere outside of the Indian subcontinent is APU'S COURSE OF HOME STUDY FOR WOULD-BE ENTREPENEURS. In 17 easy-to-understand chapters, the course covers everything you need to know in order to liberate yourself from the dismal life of a wage slave.

Topics include:

• **"How Many Lottery Tickets Would You Care to Purchase, Sir or Madame?"** and other money-making questions with which to badger your customers.

• **Turning Video Games into a Profit Center.** Includes simple instructions for resetting 30 popular models so they will no longer give free games.

• **Your Gun vs. His:** When to Freeze, When to Fire.

• **From Simple Geometric Shapes to Incarceration:** Learning to Draw Robbery Suspects in Your Spare Time.

• **2¢ of Flavoring and a Penny's Worth of Ice:** The Slushie Miracle.

• Special chapter by noted psychologist Dr. Marvin Monroe, **"Stress Reduction for Convenience Store Operators,"** will hone your skills in dealing with the retail public.

You will find all this and many other closely guarded secrets of the retail trade in this program. By studying diligently the information provided to you, you could perhaps find yourself one day in a position of public trust such as my own. Good luck!

LOOK! AT WHAT YOU GET!

MY SECURITY CAMERA IS QUICK — THE THRILLING LIFE OF A CONVENIENCE STORE OWNER

• **385-page book, MY SECURITY CAMERA IS QUICK: THE THRILLING LIFE OF A CONVENIENCE STORE OWNER,** written in Apu's own inimitable literary style!

• **Life-size photo of uniformed policeman** to place next to pastry display. Deterence value incalculable!

• **Large-print, easy-to-read ruler** to place at side of door. Most useful for determining height of fleeing suspects!

ACT NOW and receive this most handy brochure **FREE!**

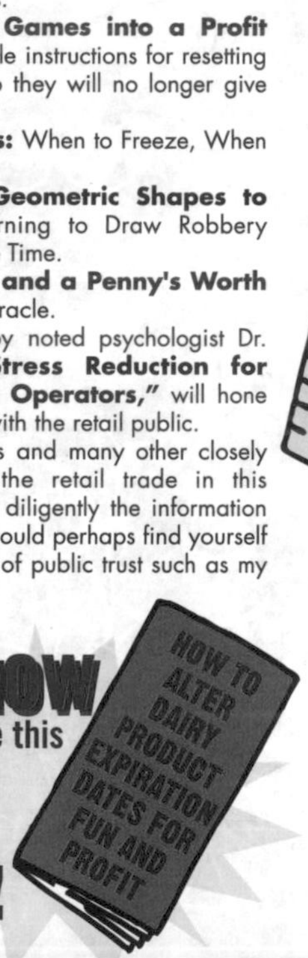

HOW TO ALTER DAIRY PRODUCT EXPIRATION DATES FOR FUN AND PROFIT

YES! Tell me more about the world of wonder that awaits me as proprietor of my own small business!

Name:_____

Street:_____

City:_____ State:_____ Zip_____

I understand that if I am not completey satisfied, it is my own damn problem.

FOR FASTER SERVICE, CALL

(900) QUIZ-APU

95¢ a minute, 20-minute minimum

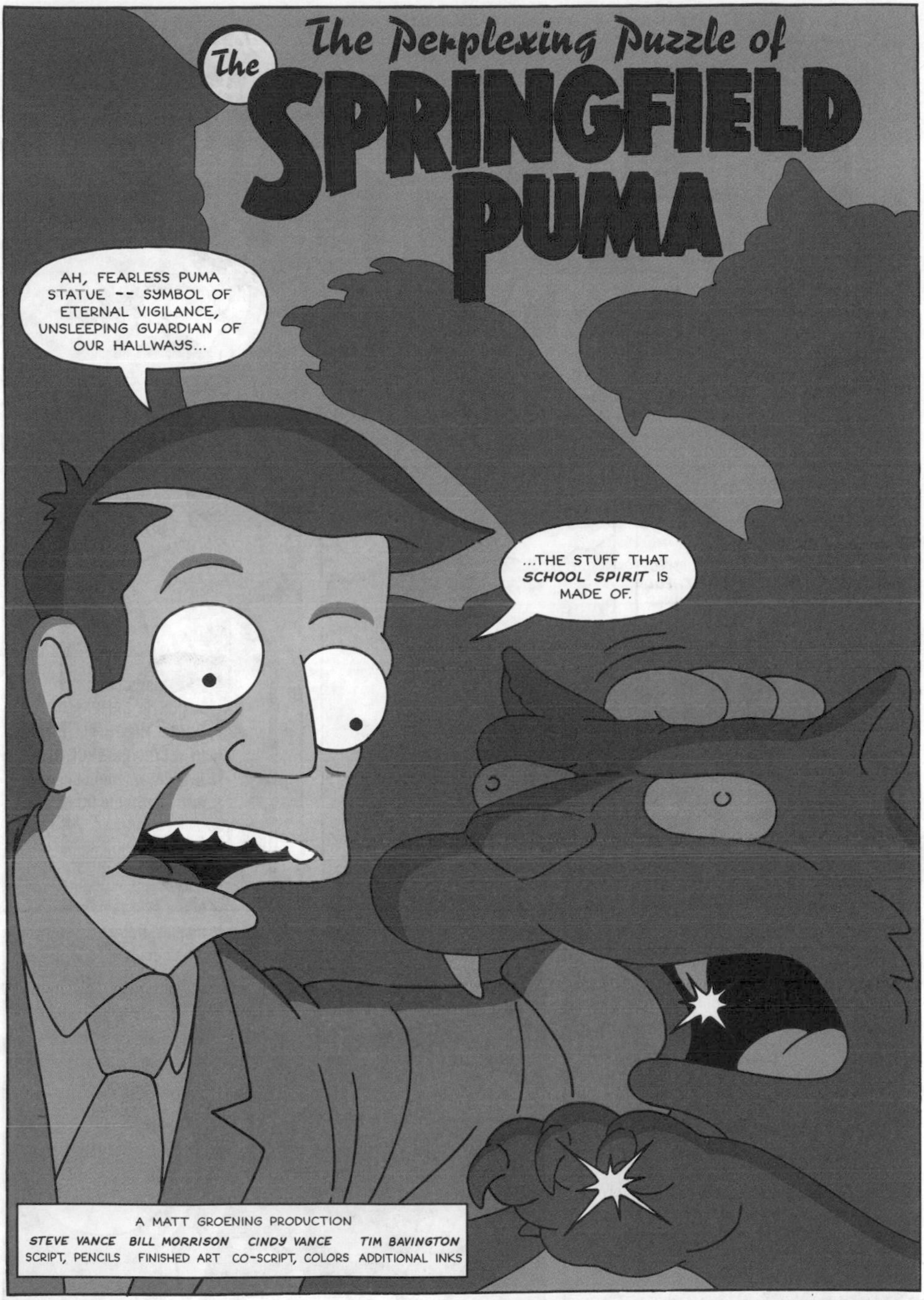
The Perplexing Puzzle of The SPRINGFIELD PUMA
AH, FEARLESS PUMA STATUE -- SYMBOL OF ETERNAL VIGILANCE, UNSLEEPING GUARDIAN OF OUR HALLWAYS...
...THE STUFF THAT SCHOOL SPIRIT IS MADE OF.
A MATT GROENING PRODUCTION
STEVE VANCE SCRIPT, PENCILS
BILL MORRISON FINISHED ART
CINDY VANCE CO-SCRIPT, COLORS
TIM BAVINGTON ADDITIONAL INKS

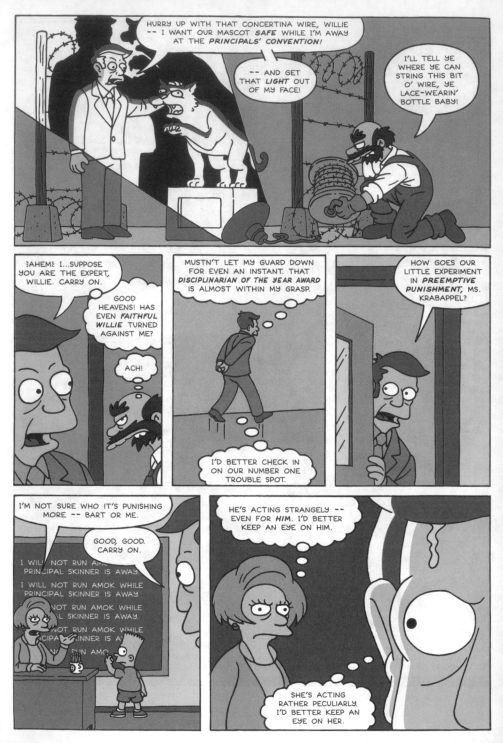

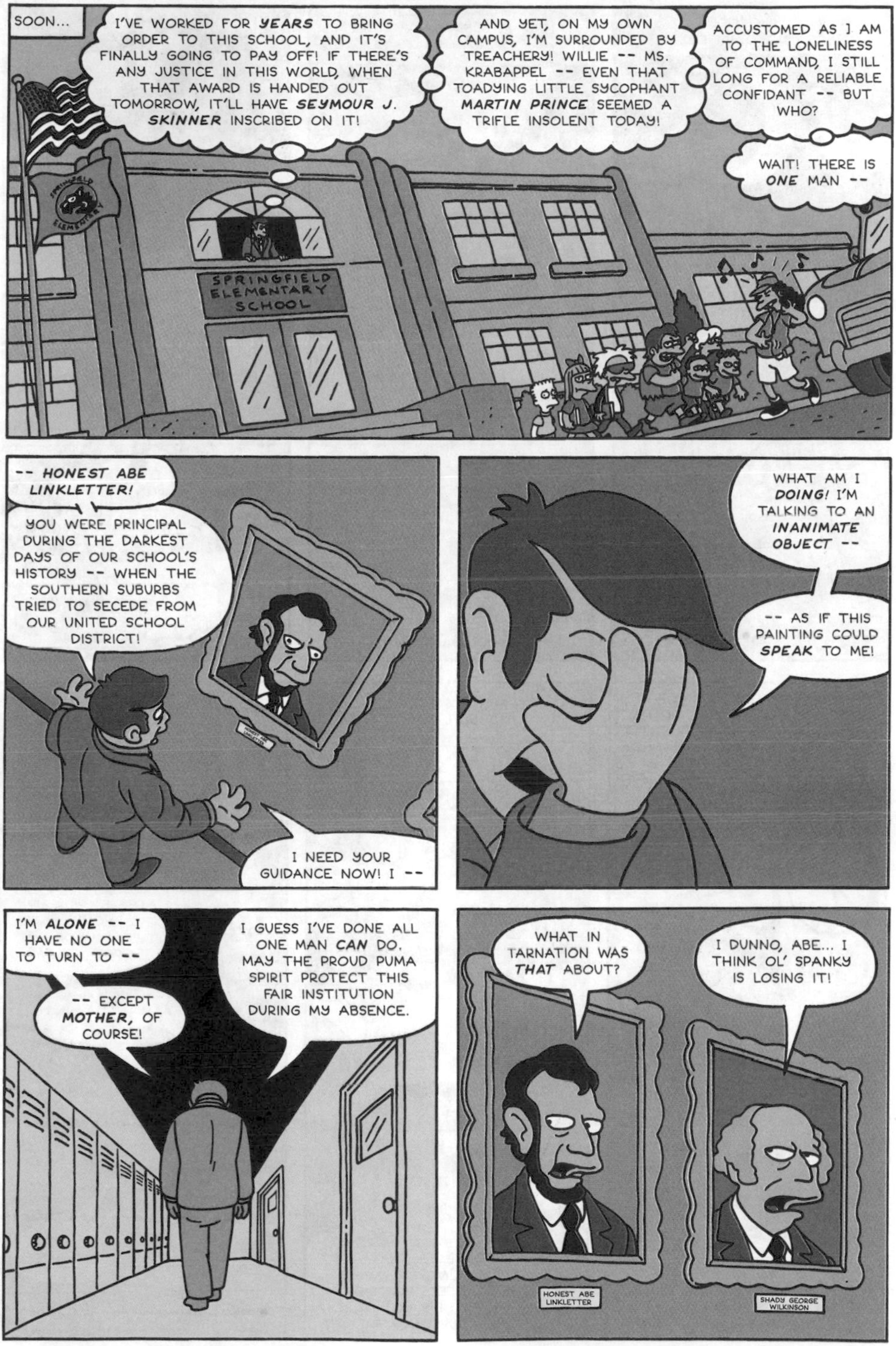
SOON...
I'VE WORKED FOR **YEARS** TO BRING ORDER TO THIS SCHOOL, AND IT'S FINALLY GOING TO PAY OFF! IF THERE'S ANY JUSTICE IN THIS WORLD, WHEN THAT AWARD IS HANDED OUT TOMORROW, IT'LL HAVE **SEYMOUR J. SKINNER** INSCRIBED ON IT!
AND YET, ON MY OWN CAMPUS, I'M SURROUNDED BY TREACHERY! WILLIE -- MS. KRABAPPEL -- EVEN THAT TOADYING LITTLE SYCOPHANT **MARTIN PRINCE** SEEMED A TRIFLE INSOLENT TODAY!
ACCUSTOMED AS I AM TO THE LONELINESS OF COMMAND, I STILL LONG FOR A RELIABLE CONFIDANT -- BUT WHO?
WAIT! THERE IS **ONE** MAN --
SPRINGFIELD ELEMENTARY
SPRINGFIELD ELEMENTARY SCHOOL
-- **HONEST ABE LINKLETTER!**
YOU WERE PRINCIPAL DURING THE DARKEST DAYS OF OUR SCHOOL'S HISTORY -- WHEN THE SOUTHERN SUBURBS TRIED TO SECEDE FROM OUR UNITED SCHOOL DISTRICT!
I NEED YOUR GUIDANCE NOW! I --
WHAT AM I **DOING!** I'M TALKING TO AN **INANIMATE OBJECT** --
-- AS IF THIS PAINTING COULD **SPEAK** TO ME!
I'M **ALONE** -- I HAVE NO ONE TO TURN TO --
-- EXCEPT **MOTHER,** OF COURSE!
I GUESS I'VE DONE ALL ONE MAN **CAN** DO. MAY THE PROUD PUMA SPIRIT PROTECT THIS FAIR INSTITUTION DURING MY ABSENCE.
WHAT IN TARNATION WAS **THAT** ABOUT?
I DUNNO, ABE... I THINK OL' SPANKY IS LOSING IT!
HONEST ABE LINKLETTER
SHADY GEORGE WILKINSON

LATER, AS DARKNESS DESCENDS ON SPRINGFIELD...

KREEK

SPRINGFIELD ELEMENTARY SCHOOL

TAK TAK TAK

TAK TAK TAK TAK TAK TAK TAK TAK

IT IS SEVERAL MINUTES PAST THE HOUR AT WHICH *JIMBO, DOLPH,* AND *KEARNY* HABITUALLY ENTER THIS ESTABLISHMENT TO BADGER MY CUSTOMERS!

PERHAPS THEY HAVE ELECTED TO PERFORM THEIR ACTS OF MAYHEM *ELSEWHERE!*

Time for Duff

:SIGH: WITHOUT THEIR PATRONAGE, I FEAR I WILL FAIL TO MEET MY *SQUISHEE SALES QUOTA!*

MARTIN, IT'S 7:30. YOU --

SPRINGFIELD PUBLIC LIBRARY

BIOG ALPH

HE'S *NOT HERE!* STRANGE -- THAT LITTLE PRIG *NEVER* LEAVES BEFORE CLOSING TIME! I DO HOPE HE'S NOT *ILL* -- HE'S OUR *ONLY PATRON.*

-- LEAVE YOUR MESSAGE AT THE SOUND OF THE BEEP.

H'LO, EDNA?

EDNA?!

EDNA, IF YOU'RE THERE, PICK UP THE PHONE -- I'M READY FOR A *GOOD TIME!*

FOR A GOOD TIME CALL EDNA K. 555-1776

:BELCH:

74

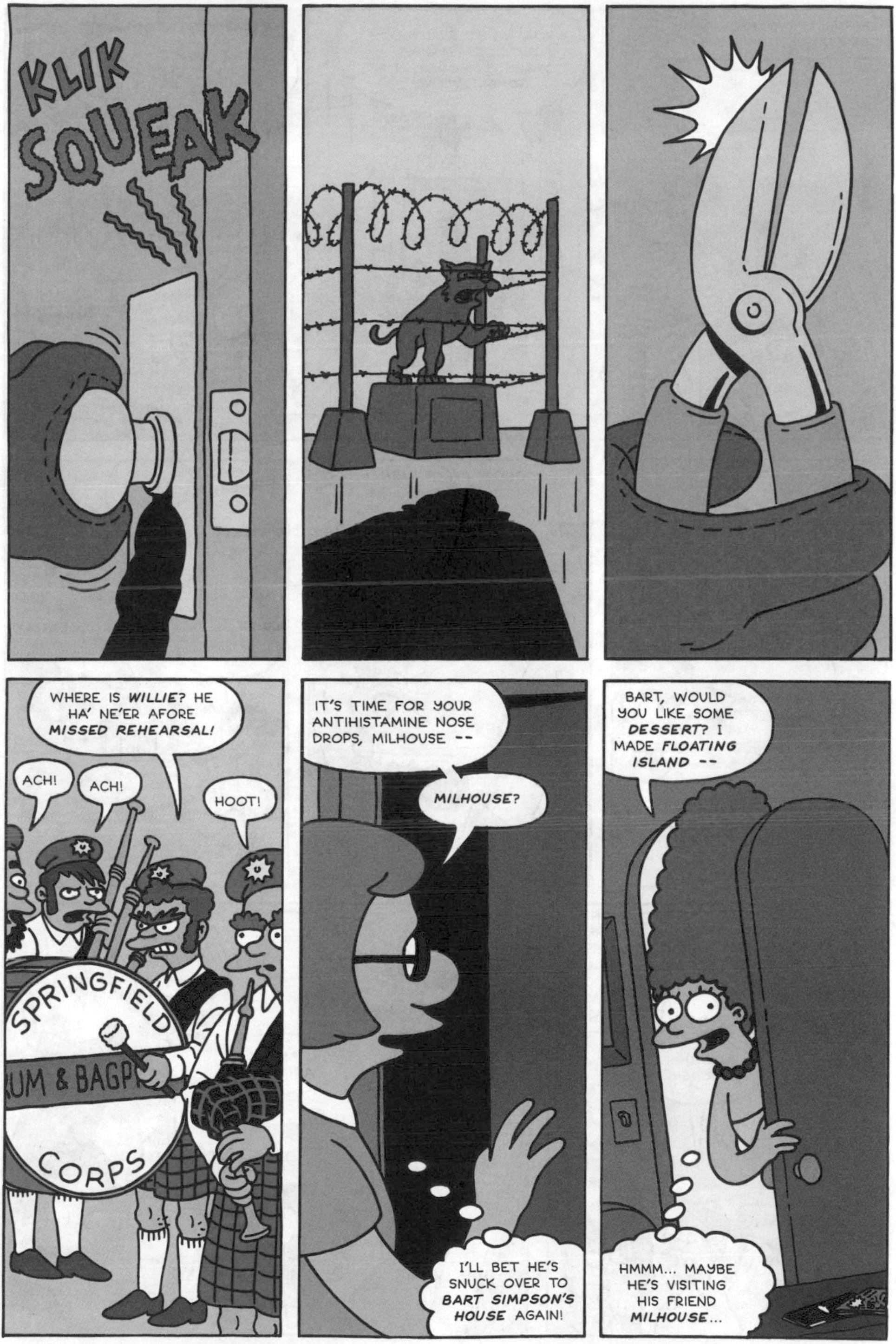
KLIK
SQUEAK
WHERE IS *WILLIE*? HE HA' NE'ER AFORE *MISSED REHEARSAL!*
ACH!
ACH!
HOOT!
SPRINGFIELD
RUM & BAGPI
CORPS
IT'S TIME FOR YOUR ANTIHISTAMINE NOSE DROPS, MILHOUSE --
MILHOUSE?
I'LL BET HE'S SNUCK OVER TO *BART SIMPSON'S HOUSE* AGAIN!
BART, WOULD YOU LIKE SOME *DESSERT?* I MADE *FLOATING ISLAND* --
HMMM... MAYBE HE'S VISITING HIS FRIEND *MILHOUSE...*

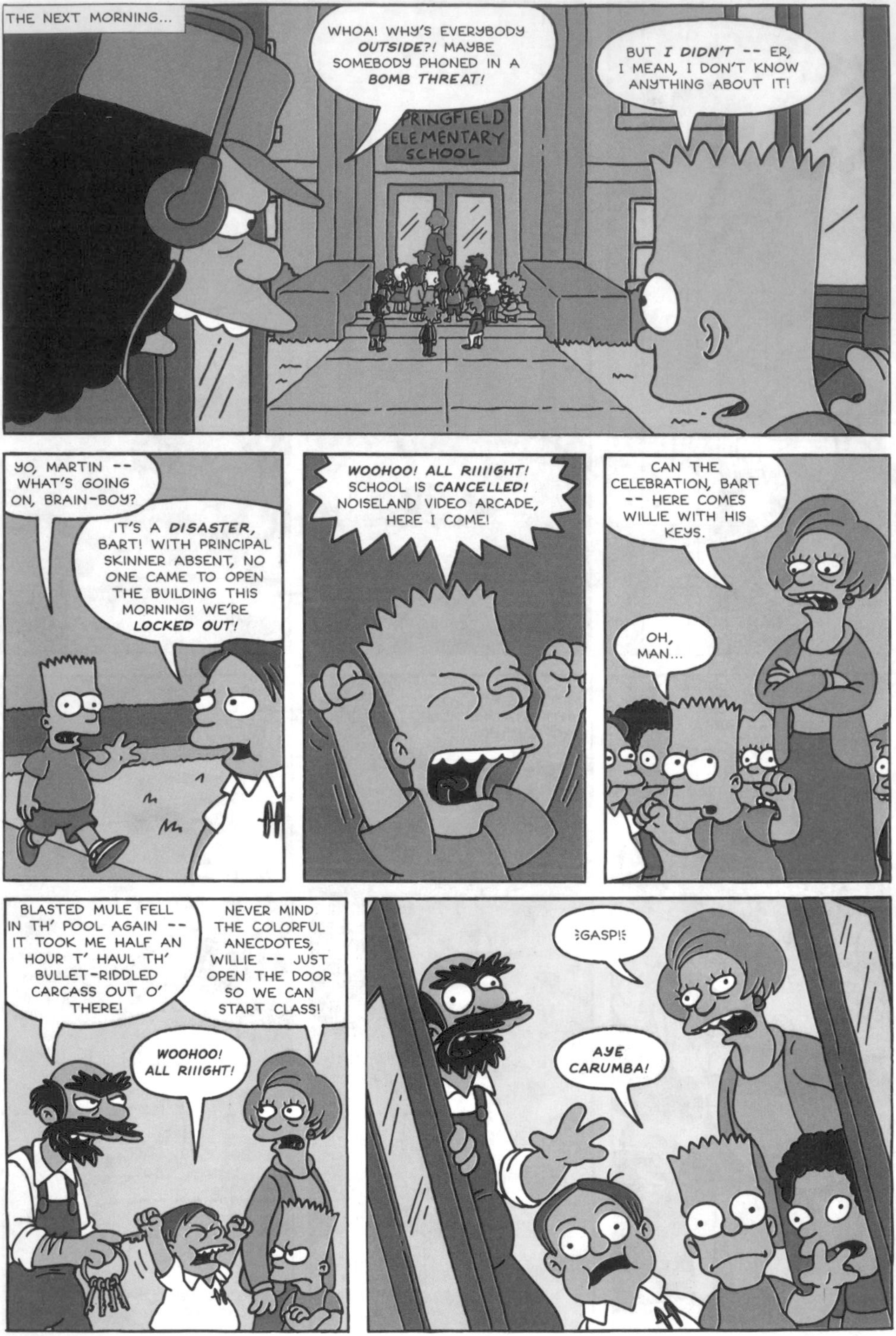
THE NEXT MORNING...
WHOA! WHY'S EVERYBODY *OUTSIDE*?! MAYBE SOMEBODY PHONED IN A *BOMB THREAT!*
SPRINGFIELD ELEMENTARY SCHOOL
BUT *I DIDN'T* -- ER, I MEAN, I DON'T KNOW ANYTHING ABOUT IT!
YO, MARTIN -- WHAT'S GOING ON, BRAIN-BOY?
IT'S A *DISASTER,* BART! WITH PRINCIPAL SKINNER ABSENT, NO ONE CAME TO OPEN THE BUILDING THIS MORNING! WE'RE *LOCKED OUT!*
WOOHOO! ALL RIIIGHT! SCHOOL IS *CANCELLED!* NOISELAND VIDEO ARCADE, HERE I COME!
CAN THE CELEBRATION, BART -- HERE COMES WILLIE WITH HIS KEYS.
OH, MAN...
BLASTED MULE FELL IN TH' POOL AGAIN -- IT TOOK ME HALF AN HOUR T' HAUL TH' BULLET-RIDDLED CARCASS OUT O' THERE!
NEVER MIND THE COLORFUL ANECDOTES, WILLIE -- JUST OPEN THE DOOR SO WE CAN START CLASS!
WOOHOO! ALL RIIIGHT!
GASP!
AYE CARUMBA!

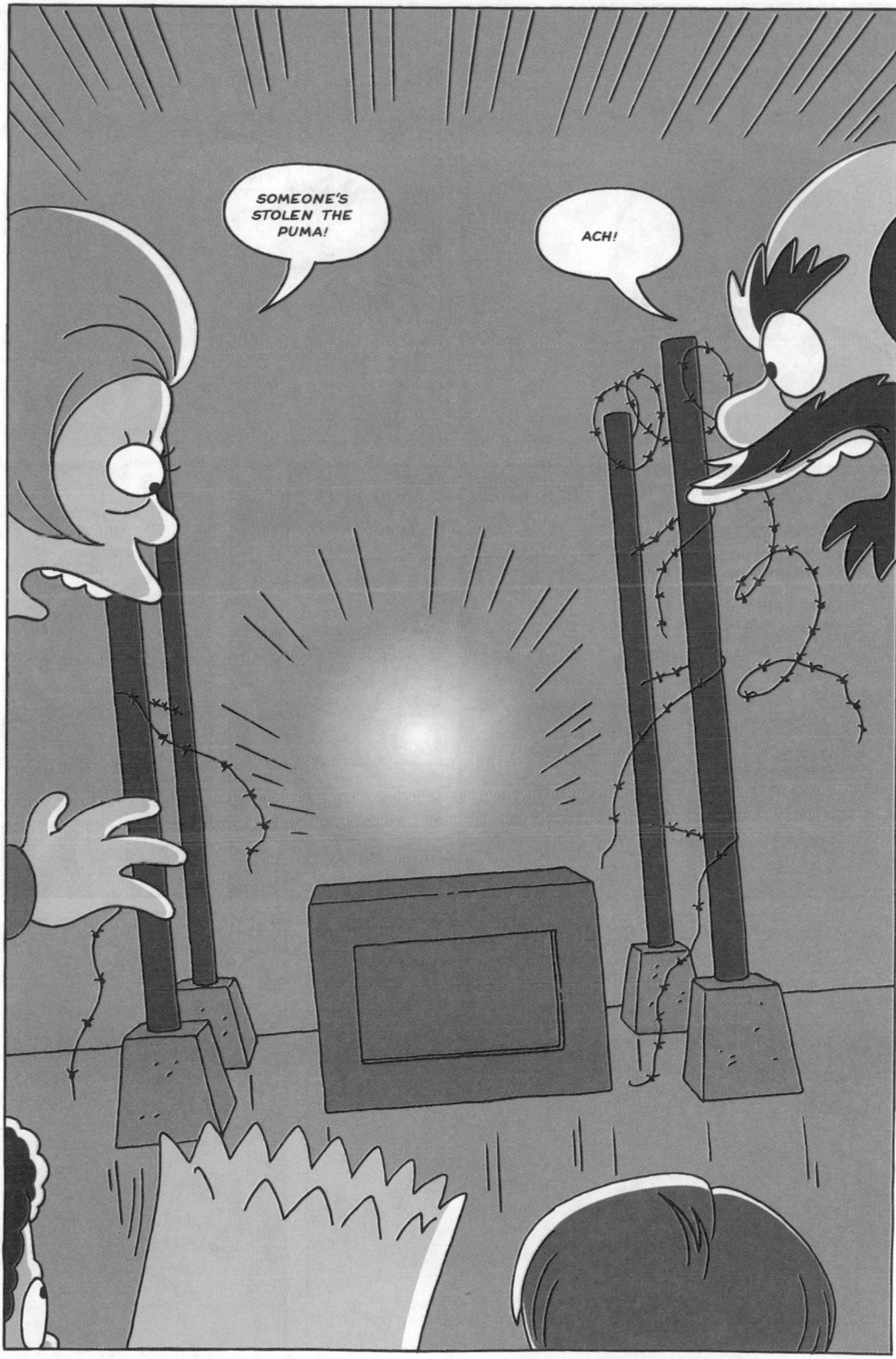
SOMEONE'S STOLEN THE PUMA!
ACH!

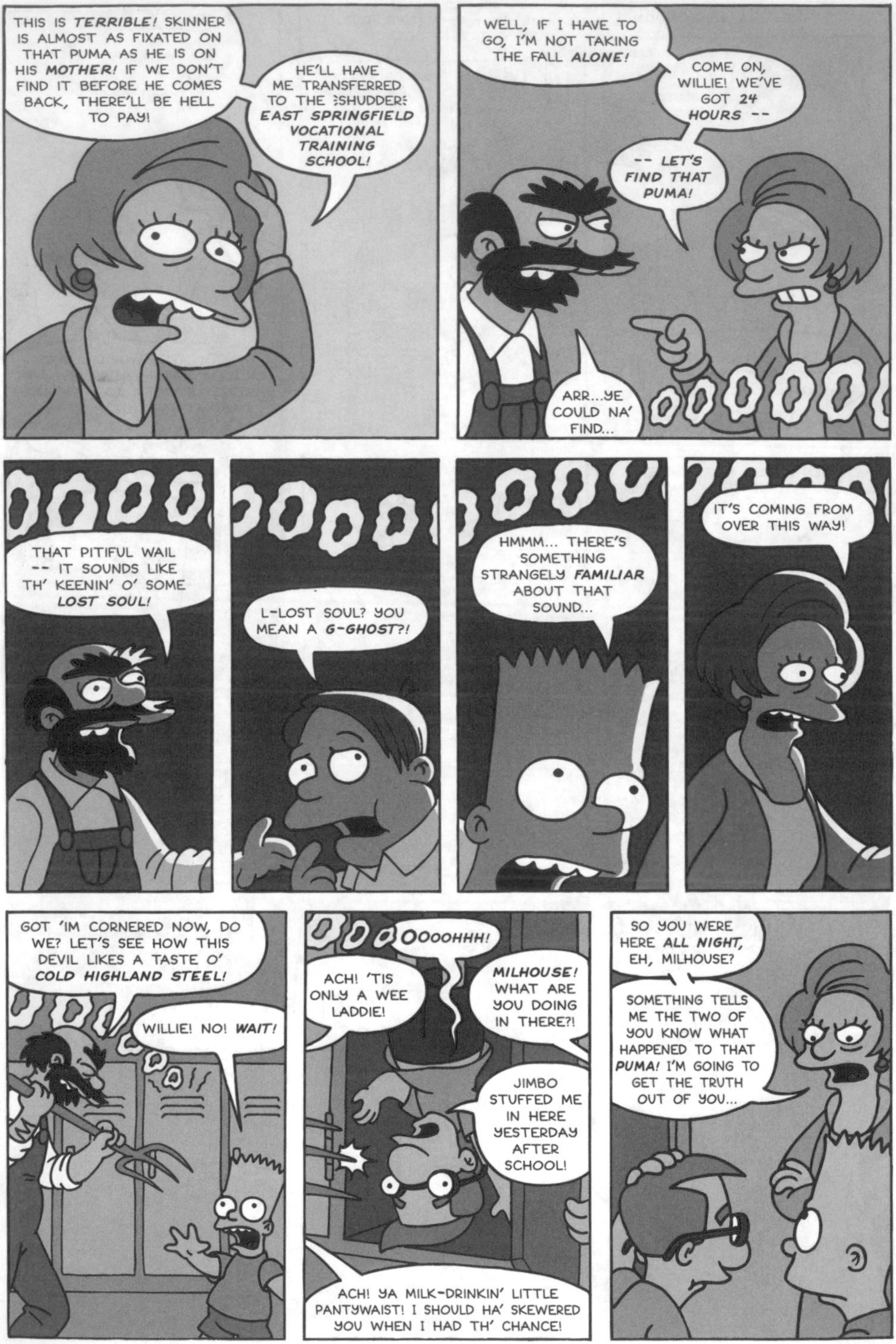

THIS IS *TERRIBLE!* SKINNER IS ALMOST AS FIXATED ON THAT PUMA AS HE IS ON HIS *MOTHER!* IF WE DON'T FIND IT BEFORE HE COMES BACK, THERE'LL BE HELL TO PAY!
HE'LL HAVE ME TRANSFERRED TO THE ⁝SHUDDER⁝ *EAST SPRINGFIELD VOCATIONAL TRAINING SCHOOL!*
WELL, IF I HAVE TO GO, I'M NOT TAKING THE FALL *ALONE!*
COME ON, WILLIE! WE'VE GOT *24 HOURS --*
-- LET'S FIND THAT PUMA!
ARR...YE COULD NA' FIND...
THAT PITIFUL WAIL -- IT SOUNDS LIKE TH' KEENIN' O' SOME *LOST SOUL!*
L-LOST SOUL? YOU MEAN A *G-GHOST?!*
HMMM... THERE'S SOMETHING STRANGELY *FAMILIAR* ABOUT THAT SOUND...
IT'S COMING FROM OVER THIS WAY!
GOT 'IM CORNERED NOW, DO WE? LET'S SEE HOW THIS DEVIL LIKES A TASTE O' *COLD HIGHLAND STEEL!*
WILLIE! NO! *WAIT!*
OOOOHHH!
ACH! 'TIS ONLY A WEE LADDIE!
MILHOUSE! WHAT ARE YOU DOING IN THERE?!
JIMBO STUFFED ME IN HERE YESTERDAY AFTER SCHOOL!
ACH! YA MILK-DRINKIN' LITTLE PANTYWAIST! I SHOULD HA' SKEWERED YOU WHEN I HAD TH' CHANCE!
SO YOU WERE HERE *ALL NIGHT,* EH, MILHOUSE?
SOMETHING TELLS ME THE TWO OF YOU KNOW WHAT HAPPENED TO THAT *PUMA!* I'M GOING TO GET THE TRUTH OUT OF YOU...

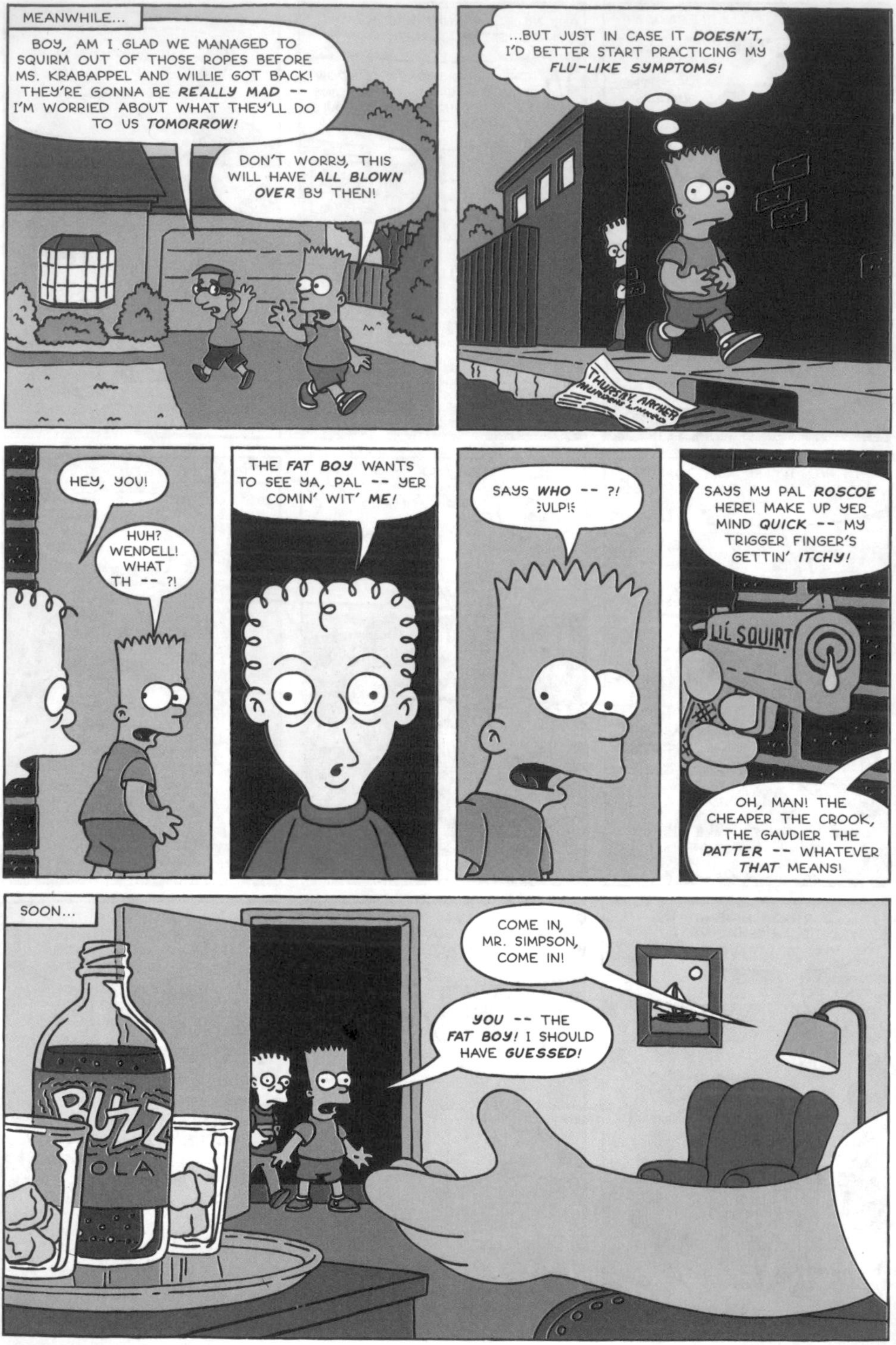

MEANWHILE...
BOY, AM I GLAD WE MANAGED TO SQUIRM OUT OF THOSE ROPES BEFORE MS. KRABAPPEL AND WILLIE GOT BACK! THEY'RE GONNA BE REALLY MAD -- I'M WORRIED ABOUT WHAT THEY'LL DO TO US TOMORROW!
DON'T WORRY, THIS WILL HAVE ALL BLOWN OVER BY THEN!
...BUT JUST IN CASE IT DOESN'T, I'D BETTER START PRACTICING MY FLU-LIKE SYMPTOMS!
THURSBY, ARCHER MURDERS LINKED
HEY, YOU!
HUH? WENDELL! WHAT TH -- ?!
THE FAT BOY WANTS TO SEE YA, PAL -- YER COMIN' WIT' ME!
SAYS WHO -- ?!
ULP!
SAYS MY PAL ROSCOE HERE! MAKE UP YER MIND QUICK -- MY TRIGGER FINGER'S GETTIN' ITCHY!
LIL SQUIRT
OH, MAN! THE CHEAPER THE CROOK, THE GAUDIER THE PATTER -- WHATEVER THAT MEANS!
SOON...
COME IN, MR. SIMPSON, COME IN!
YOU -- THE FAT BOY! I SHOULD HAVE GUESSED!
BUZZ COLA

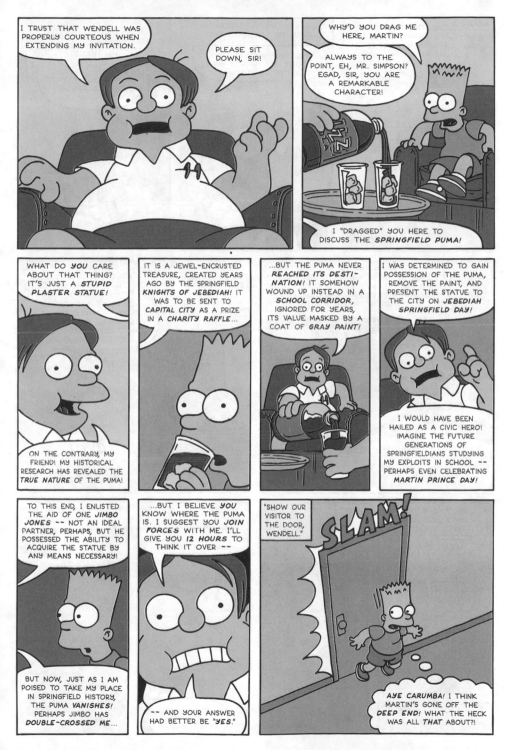

I TRUST THAT WENDELL WAS PROPERLY COURTEOUS WHEN EXTENDING MY INVITATION.

PLEASE SIT DOWN, SIR!

WHY'D YOU DRAG ME HERE, MARTIN?

ALWAYS TO THE POINT, EH, MR. SIMPSON? EGAD, SIR, YOU ARE A REMARKABLE CHARACTER!

I "DRAGGED" YOU HERE TO DISCUSS THE *SPRINGFIELD PUMA!*

WHAT DO *YOU* CARE ABOUT THAT THING? IT'S JUST A *STUPID PLASTER STATUE!*

ON THE CONTRARY, MY FRIEND! MY HISTORICAL RESEARCH HAS REVEALED THE *TRUE NATURE* OF THE PUMA!

IT IS A JEWEL-ENCRUSTED TREASURE, CREATED YEARS AGO BY THE SPRINGFIELD *KNIGHTS OF JEBEDIAH!* IT WAS TO BE SENT TO *CAPITAL CITY* AS A PRIZE IN A *CHARITY RAFFLE...*

...BUT THE PUMA NEVER *REACHED ITS DESTI- NATION!* IT SOMEHOW WOUND UP INSTEAD IN A *SCHOOL CORRIDOR,* IGNORED FOR YEARS, ITS VALUE MASKED BY A COAT OF *GRAY PAINT!*

I WAS DETERMINED TO GAIN POSSESSION OF THE PUMA, REMOVE THE PAINT, AND PRESENT THE STATUE TO THE CITY ON *JEBEDIAH SPRINGFIELD DAY!*

I WOULD HAVE BEEN HAILED AS A CIVIC HERO! IMAGINE THE FUTURE GENERATIONS OF SPRINGFIELDIANS STUDYING MY EXPLOITS IN SCHOOL -- PERHAPS EVEN CELEBRATING *MARTIN PRINCE DAY!*

TO THIS END, I ENLISTED THE AID OF ONE *JIMBO JONES* -- NOT AN IDEAL PARTNER, PERHAPS, BUT HE POSSESSED THE ABILITY TO ACQUIRE THE STATUE BY ANY MEANS NECESSARY!

BUT NOW, JUST AS I AM POISED TO TAKE MY PLACE IN SPRINGFIELD HISTORY, THE PUMA *VANISHES!* PERHAPS JIMBO HAS *DOUBLE-CROSSED ME...*

...BUT I BELIEVE *YOU* KNOW WHERE THE PUMA IS. I SUGGEST YOU *JOIN FORCES* WITH ME. I'LL GIVE YOU *12 HOURS* TO THINK IT OVER --

-- AND YOUR ANSWER HAD BETTER BE *"YES."*

"SHOW OUR VISITOR TO THE DOOR, WENDELL."

SLAM!

AYE CARUMBA! I THINK MARTIN'S GONE OFF THE *DEEP END!* WHAT THE HECK WAS ALL *THAT* ABOUT?!

83

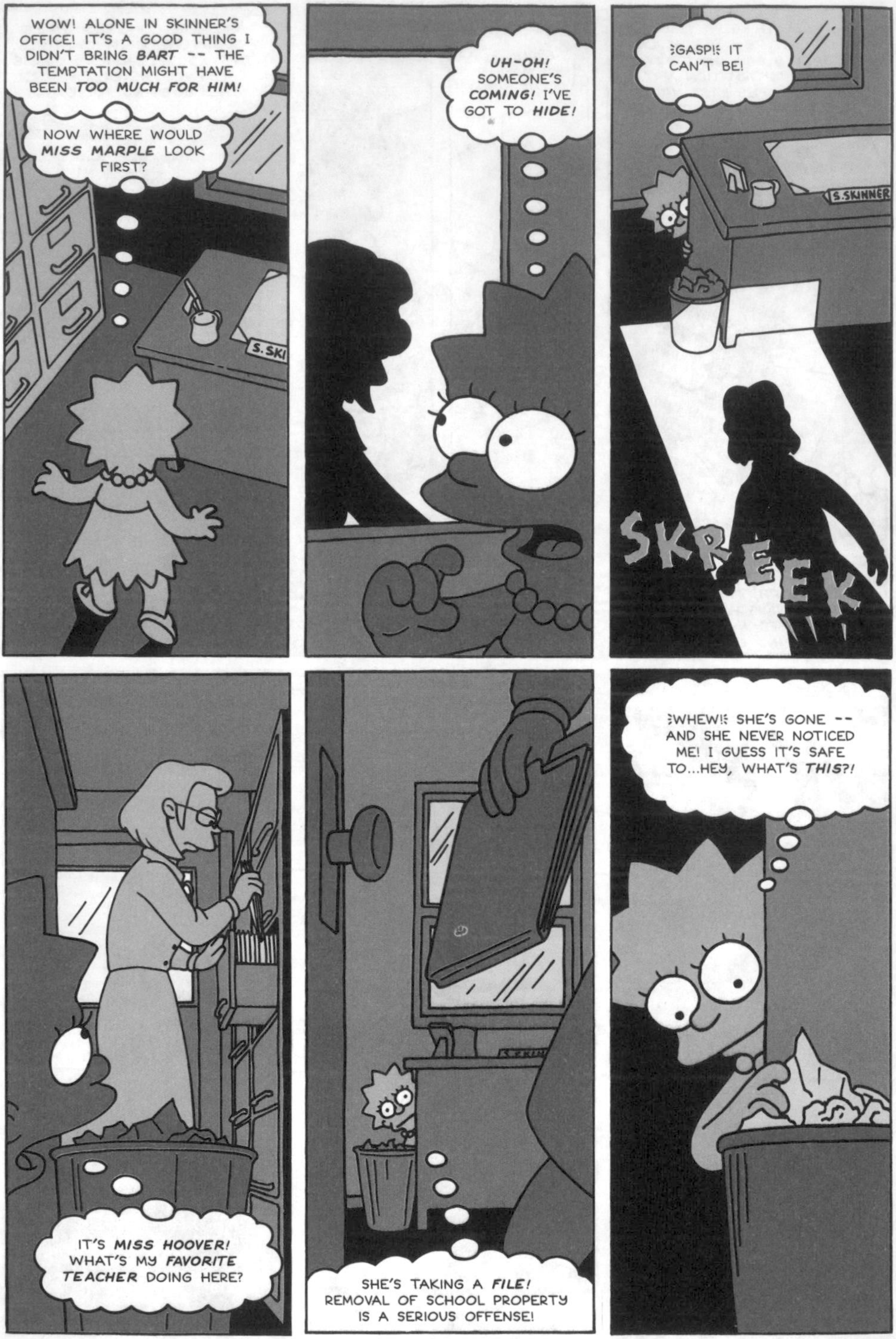
WOW! ALONE IN SKINNER'S OFFICE! IT'S A GOOD THING I DIDN'T BRING BART -- THE TEMPTATION MIGHT HAVE BEEN TOO MUCH FOR HIM!
NOW WHERE WOULD MISS MARPLE LOOK FIRST?
S. SKI
UH-OH! SOMEONE'S COMING! I'VE GOT TO HIDE!
GASP! IT CAN'T BE!
S.SKINNER
SKREEEK
IT'S MISS HOOVER! WHAT'S MY FAVORITE TEACHER DOING HERE?
SHE'S TAKING A FILE! REMOVAL OF SCHOOL PROPERTY IS A SERIOUS OFFENSE!
WHEW! SHE'S GONE -- AND SHE NEVER NOTICED ME! I GUESS IT'S SAFE TO...HEY, WHAT'S THIS?!

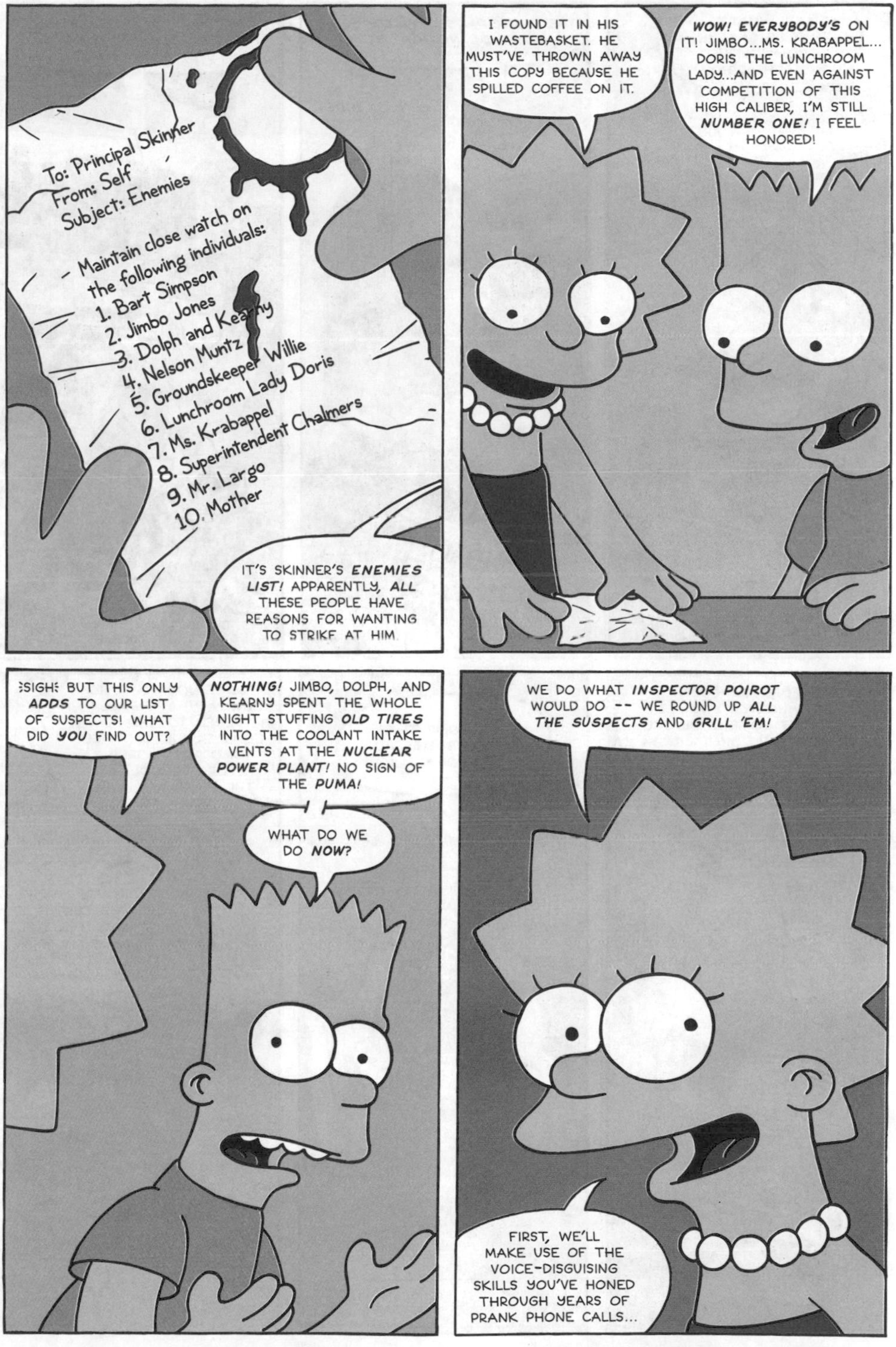
To: Principal Skinner
From: Self
Subject: Enemies
Maintain close watch on the following individuals:
1. Bart Simpson
2. Jimbo Jones
3. Dolph and Kearny
4. Nelson Muntz
5. Groundskeeper Willie
6. Lunchroom Lady Doris
7. Ms. Krabappel
8. Superintendent Chalmers
9. Mr. Largo
10. Mother
IT'S SKINNER'S ENEMIES LIST! APPARENTLY, ALL THESE PEOPLE HAVE REASONS FOR WANTING TO STRIKE AT HIM.
I FOUND IT IN HIS WASTEBASKET. HE MUST'VE THROWN AWAY THIS COPY BECAUSE HE SPILLED COFFEE ON IT.
WOW! EVERYBODY'S ON IT! JIMBO...MS. KRABAPPEL... DORIS THE LUNCHROOM LADY...AND EVEN AGAINST COMPETITION OF THIS HIGH CALIBER, I'M STILL NUMBER ONE! I FEEL HONORED!
:SIGH: BUT THIS ONLY ADDS TO OUR LIST OF SUSPECTS! WHAT DID YOU FIND OUT?
NOTHING! JIMBO, DOLPH, AND KEARNY SPENT THE WHOLE NIGHT STUFFING OLD TIRES INTO THE COOLANT INTAKE VENTS AT THE NUCLEAR POWER PLANT! NO SIGN OF THE PUMA!
WHAT DO WE DO NOW?
WE DO WHAT INSPECTOR POIROT WOULD DO -- WE ROUND UP ALL THE SUSPECTS AND GRILL 'EM!
FIRST, WE'LL MAKE USE OF THE VOICE-DISGUISING SKILLS YOU'VE HONED THROUGH YEARS OF PRANK PHONE CALLS...

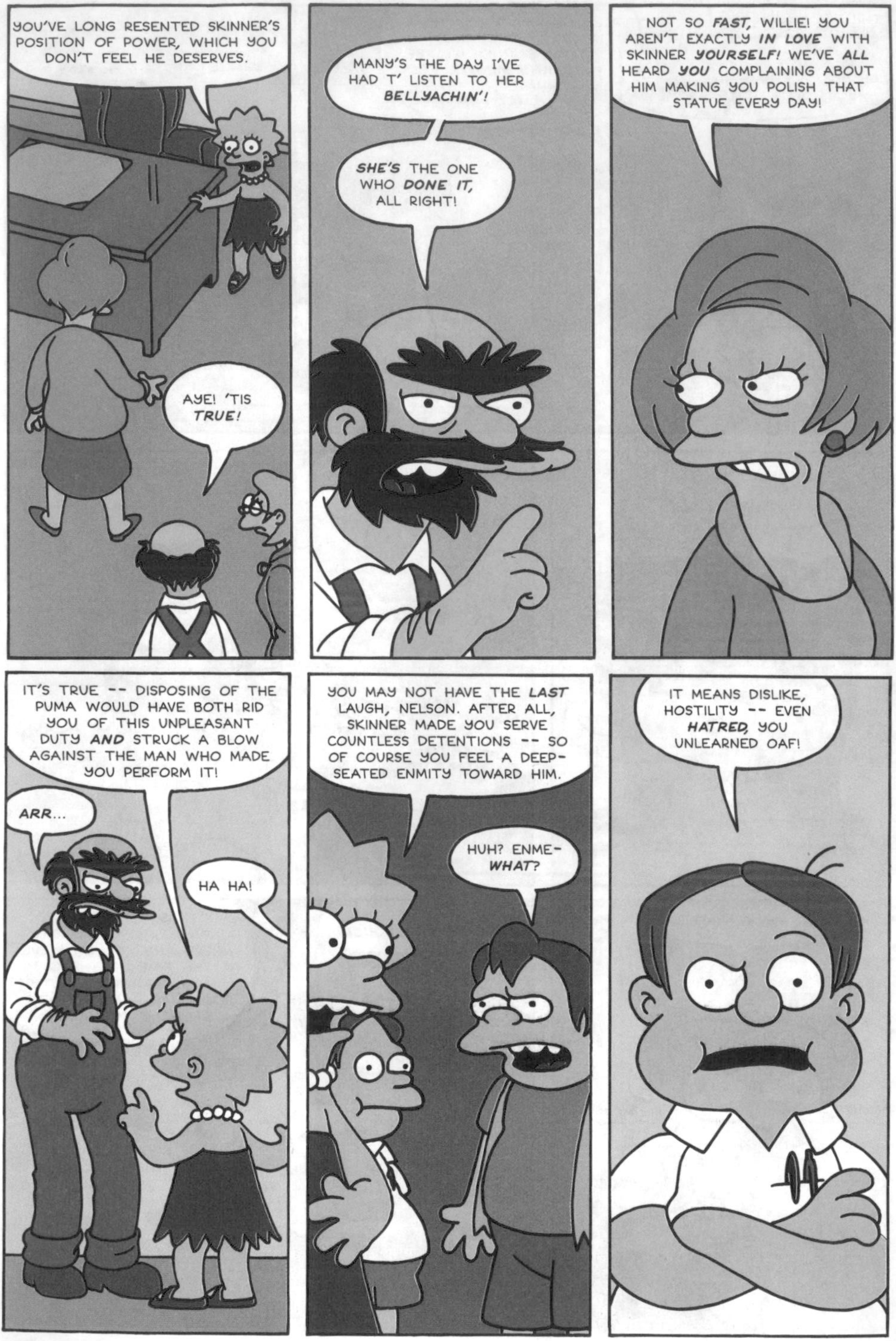
YOU'VE LONG RESENTED SKINNER'S POSITION OF POWER, WHICH YOU DON'T FEEL HE DESERVES.
AYE! 'TIS TRUE!
MANY'S THE DAY I'VE HAD T' LISTEN TO HER BELLYACHIN'!
SHE'S THE ONE WHO DONE IT, ALL RIGHT!
NOT SO FAST, WILLIE! YOU AREN'T EXACTLY IN LOVE WITH SKINNER YOURSELF! WE'VE ALL HEARD YOU COMPLAINING ABOUT HIM MAKING YOU POLISH THAT STATUE EVERY DAY!
IT'S TRUE -- DISPOSING OF THE PUMA WOULD HAVE BOTH RID YOU OF THIS UNPLEASANT DUTY AND STRUCK A BLOW AGAINST THE MAN WHO MADE YOU PERFORM IT!
ARR...
HA HA!
YOU MAY NOT HAVE THE LAST LAUGH, NELSON. AFTER ALL, SKINNER MADE YOU SERVE COUNTLESS DETENTIONS -- SO OF COURSE YOU FEEL A DEEP-SEATED ENMITY TOWARD HIM.
HUH? ENME-WHAT?
IT MEANS DISLIKE, HOSTILITY -- EVEN HATRED, YOU UNLEARNED OAF!

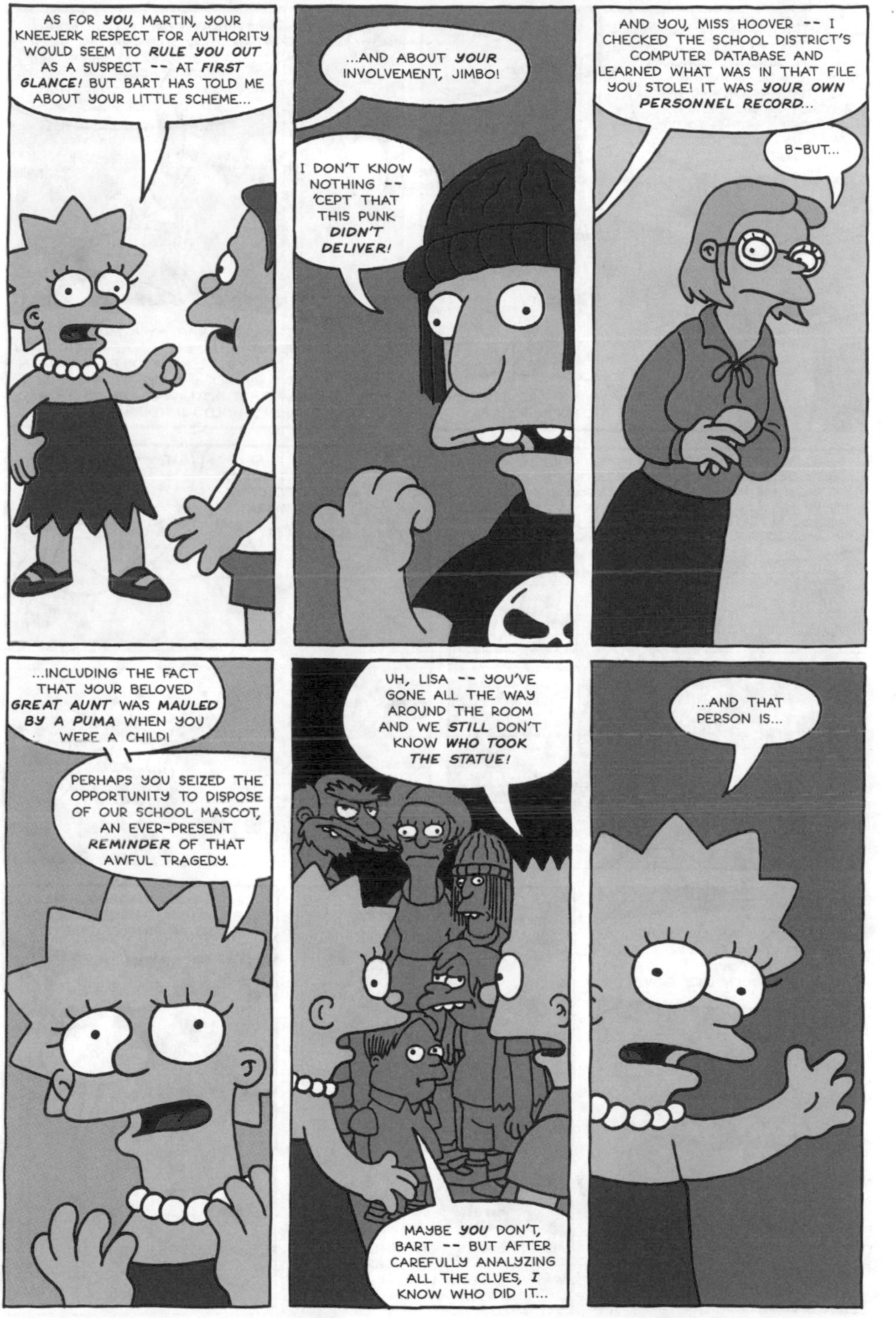
AS FOR *YOU*, MARTIN, YOUR KNEEJERK RESPECT FOR AUTHORITY WOULD SEEM TO *RULE YOU OUT* AS A SUSPECT -- AT *FIRST GLANCE!* BUT BART HAS TOLD ME ABOUT YOUR LITTLE SCHEME...
...AND ABOUT *YOUR* INVOLVEMENT, JIMBO!
I DON'T KNOW NOTHING -- 'CEPT THAT THIS PUNK *DIDN'T DELIVER!*
AND YOU, MISS HOOVER -- I CHECKED THE SCHOOL DISTRICT'S COMPUTER DATABASE AND LEARNED WHAT WAS IN THAT FILE YOU STOLE! IT WAS *YOUR OWN PERSONNEL RECORD*...
B-BUT...
...INCLUDING THE FACT THAT YOUR BELOVED *GREAT AUNT* WAS *MAULED BY A PUMA* WHEN YOU WERE A CHILD!
PERHAPS YOU SEIZED THE OPPORTUNITY TO DISPOSE OF OUR SCHOOL MASCOT, AN EVER-PRESENT *REMINDER* OF THAT AWFUL TRAGEDY.
UH, LISA -- YOU'VE GONE ALL THE WAY AROUND THE ROOM AND WE *STILL* DON'T KNOW *WHO TOOK THE STATUE!*
MAYBE *YOU* DON'T, BART -- BUT AFTER CAREFULLY ANALYZING ALL THE CLUES, *I* KNOW WHO DID IT...
...AND THAT PERSON IS...

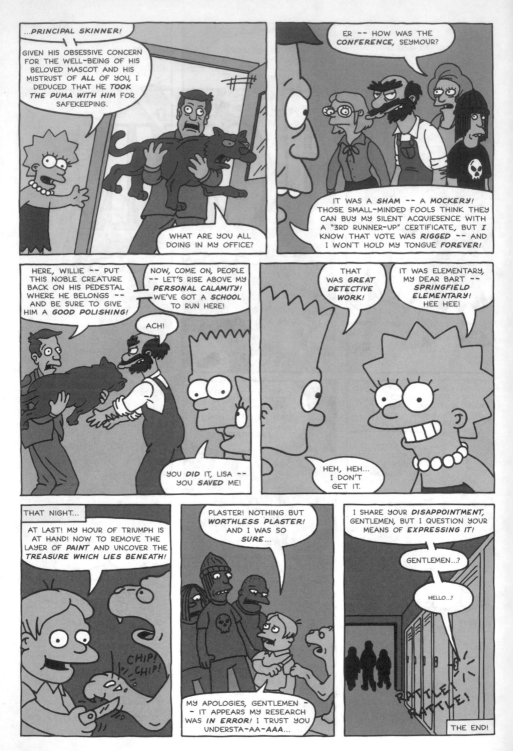

...*PRINCIPAL SKINNER!*

GIVEN HIS OBSESSIVE CONCERN FOR THE WELL-BEING OF HIS BELOVED MASCOT AND HIS MISTRUST OF **ALL OF YOU,** I DEDUCED THAT HE *TOOK THE PUMA WITH HIM* FOR SAFEKEEPING.

WHAT ARE YOU ALL DOING IN MY OFFICE?

ER -- HOW WAS THE *CONFERENCE,* SEYMOUR?

IT WAS A *SHAM* -- A *MOCKERY!* THOSE SMALL-MINDED FOOLS THINK THEY CAN BUY MY SILENT ACQUIESCENCE WITH A "3RD RUNNER-UP" CERTIFICATE, BUT *I* KNOW THAT VOTE WAS *RIGGED* -- AND I WON'T HOLD MY TONGUE *FOREVER!*

HERE, WILLIE -- PUT THIS NOBLE CREATURE BACK ON HIS PEDESTAL WHERE HE BELONGS -- AND BE SURE TO GIVE HIM A *GOOD POLISHING!*

NOW, COME ON, PEOPLE -- LET'S RISE ABOVE MY *PERSONAL CALAMITY!* WE'VE GOT A *SCHOOL* TO RUN HERE!

ACH!

YOU *DID* IT, LISA -- YOU *SAVED* ME!

THAT WAS *GREAT DETECTIVE* WORK!

IT WAS ELEMENTARY, MY DEAR BART -- *SPRINGFIELD ELEMENTARY!* HEE HEE!

HEH, HEH... I DON'T GET IT.

THAT NIGHT...

AT LAST! MY HOUR OF TRIUMPH IS AT HAND! NOW TO REMOVE THE LAYER OF *PAINT* AND UNCOVER THE *TREASURE WHICH LIES BENEATH!*

CHIP! CHIP!

PLASTER! NOTHING BUT *WORTHLESS PLASTER!* AND I WAS SO *SURE...*

MY APOLOGIES, GENTLEMEN -- IT APPEARS MY RESEARCH WAS *IN ERROR!* I TRUST YOU UNDERSTA-AA-AAA...

I SHARE YOUR *DISAPPOINTMENT,* GENTLEMEN, BUT I QUESTION YOUR MEANS OF *EXPRESSING IT!*

GENTLEMEN...?

HELLO...?

RATTLE! RATTLE!

THE END!

BONGO COMICS GROUP
KRUSTY, AGENT OF K.L.O.W.N.
BANG
MATT GROENING Morrison
© 1994 BONGO ENTERTAINMENT, INC. THE SIMPSONS ® & ™ TWENTIETH CENTURY FOX FILM CORPORATION. ALL RIGHTS RESERVED.

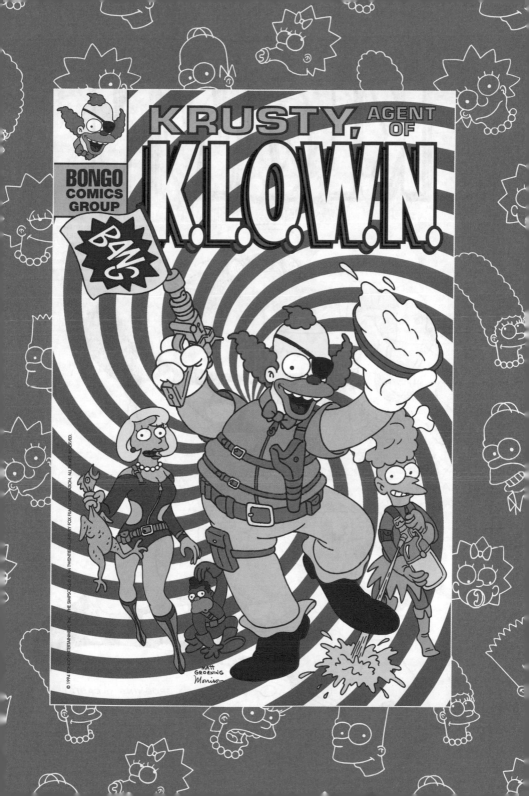

KRUSTY, AGENT OF K.L.O.W.N.

KEEPING LAW & ORDER WITH NOVELTY ITEMS

MR. TEENY -- NO! DON'T TOUCH THAT SWITCH! IT OPENS THE --
YAAAAAAA!!
WHEW! LUCKY I'M WEARIN' MY A.C.R.O.N.Y.M.* SUIT! WITH THESE WINGS, I CAN GLIDE TO SAFETY!

A GROENING ☆ CASTELLANETA
LACUSTA ☆ VANCE ☆ MORRISON
BAVINGTON ☆ VANCE PRODUCTION

*AERIAL CONTROLLED RUDDERLESS ORDNANCE NODE -- YEAH, MAN!

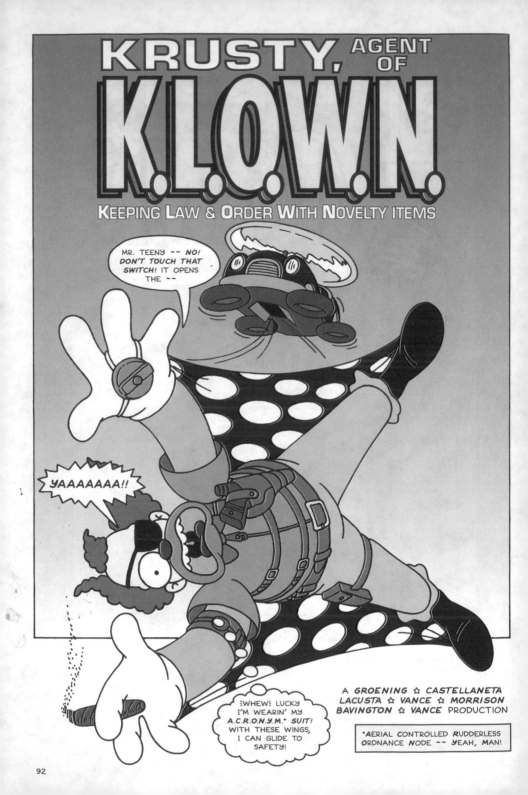

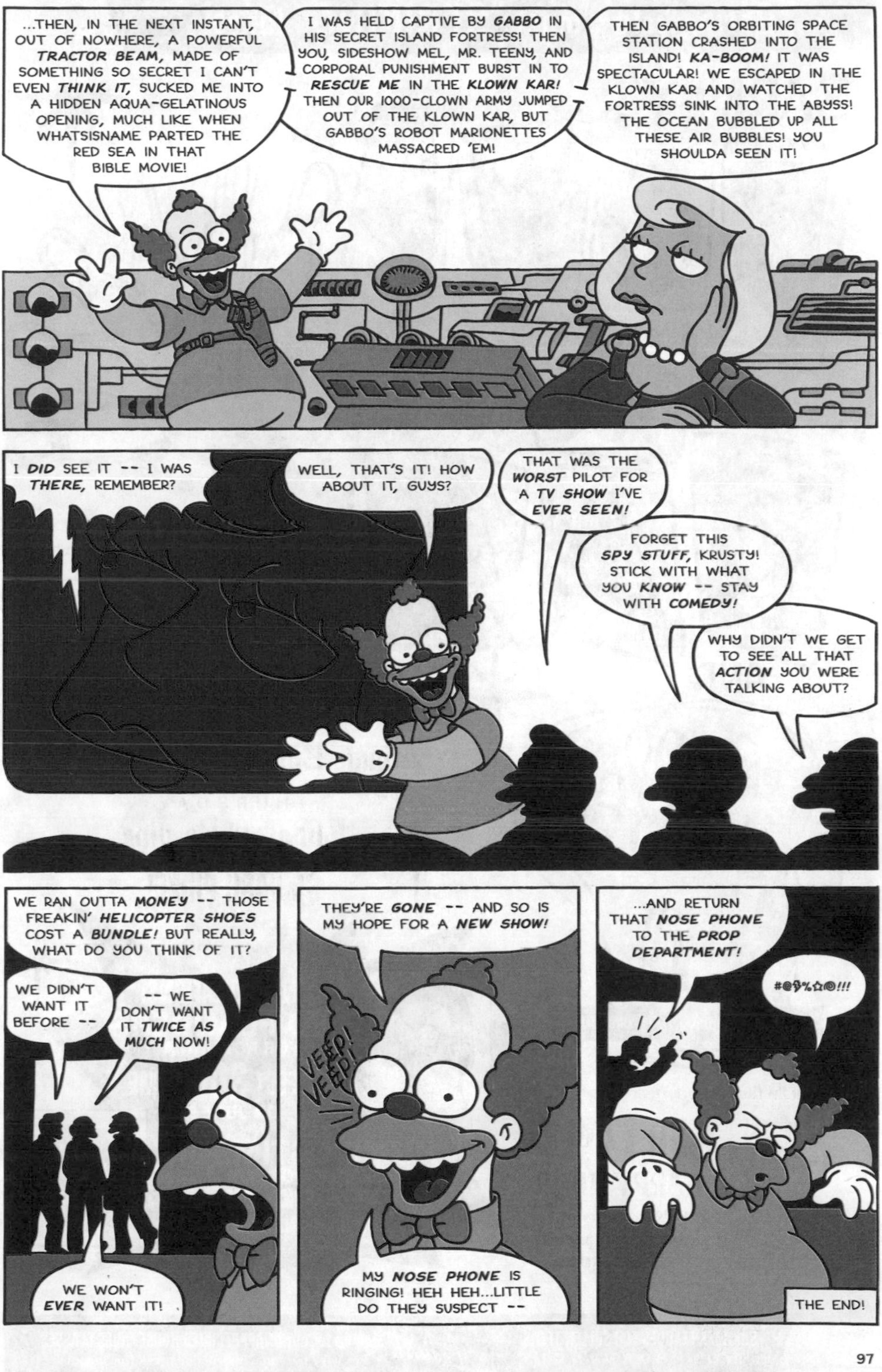
...THEN, IN THE NEXT INSTANT, OUT OF NOWHERE, A POWERFUL TRACTOR BEAM, MADE OF SOMETHING SO SECRET I CAN'T EVEN THINK IT, SUCKED ME INTO A HIDDEN AQUA-GELATINOUS OPENING, MUCH LIKE WHEN WHATSISNAME PARTED THE RED SEA IN THAT BIBLE MOVIE!
I WAS HELD CAPTIVE BY GABBO IN HIS SECRET ISLAND FORTRESS! THEN YOU, SIDESHOW MEL, MR. TEENY, AND CORPORAL PUNISHMENT BURST IN TO RESCUE ME IN THE KLOWN KAR! THEN OUR 1000-CLOWN ARMY JUMPED OUT OF THE KLOWN KAR, BUT GABBO'S ROBOT MARIONETTES MASSACRED 'EM!
THEN GABBO'S ORBITING SPACE STATION CRASHED INTO THE ISLAND! KA-BOOM! IT WAS SPECTACULAR! WE ESCAPED IN THE KLOWN KAR AND WATCHED THE FORTRESS SINK INTO THE ABYSS! THE OCEAN BUBBLED UP ALL THESE AIR BUBBLES! YOU SHOULDA SEEN IT!
I DID SEE IT -- I WAS THERE, REMEMBER?
WELL, THAT'S IT! HOW ABOUT IT, GUYS?
THAT WAS THE WORST PILOT FOR A TV SHOW I'VE EVER SEEN!
FORGET THIS SPY STUFF, KRUSTY! STICK WITH WHAT YOU KNOW -- STAY WITH COMEDY!
WHY DIDN'T WE GET TO SEE ALL THAT ACTION YOU WERE TALKING ABOUT?
WE RAN OUTTA MONEY -- THOSE FREAKIN' HELICOPTER SHOES COST A BUNDLE! BUT REALLY, WHAT DO YOU THINK OF IT?
WE DIDN'T WANT IT BEFORE --
-- WE DON'T WANT IT TWICE AS MUCH NOW!
WE WON'T EVER WANT IT!
THEY'RE GONE -- AND SO IS MY HOPE FOR A NEW SHOW!
VEEP! VEEP!
MY NOSE PHONE IS RINGING! HEH HEH...LITTLE DO THEY SUSPECT --
...AND RETURN THAT NOSE PHONE TO THE PROP DEPARTMENT!
#@$%☆@!!!
THE END!

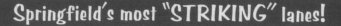

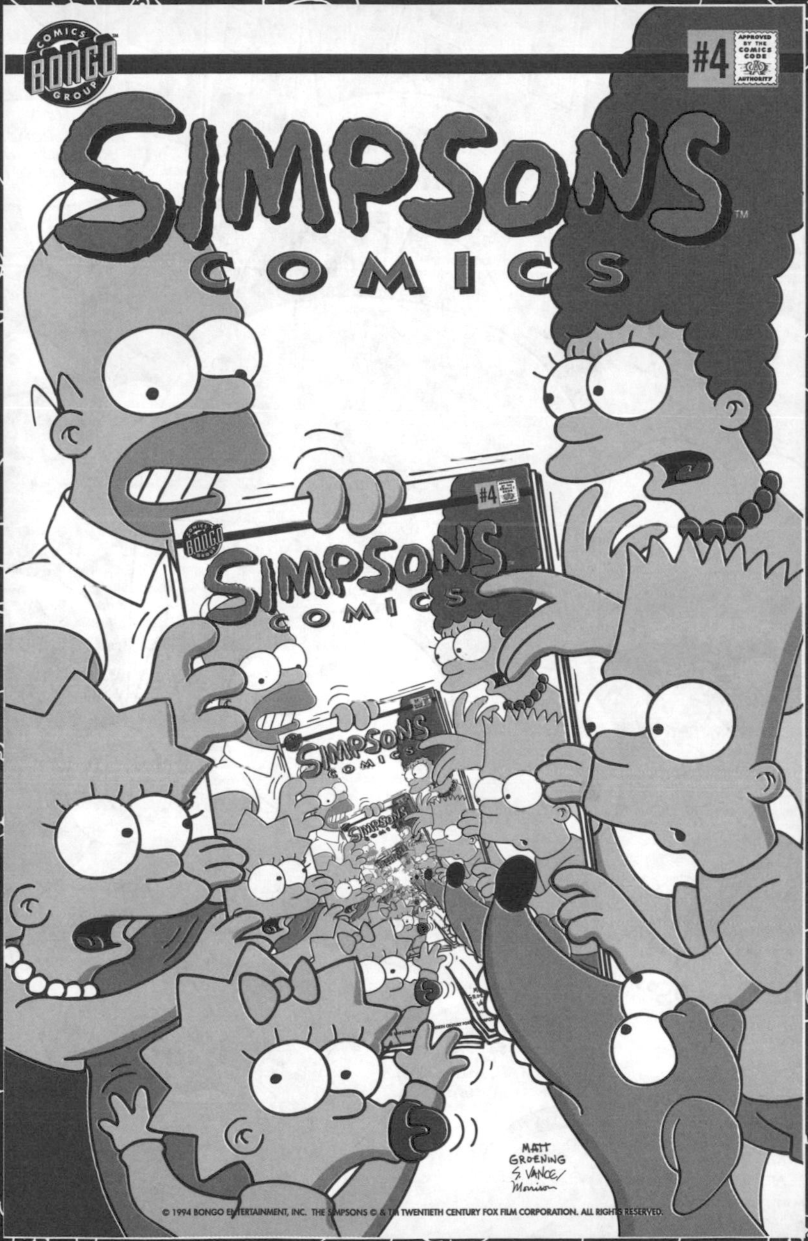

COMICS BONGO GROUP
#4
APPROVED BY THE COMICS CODE AUTHORITY
SIMPSONS COMICS
MATT GROENING S. VANCE/ Morrison
© 1994 BONGO ENTERTAINMENT, INC. THE SIMPSONS © & TM TWENTIETH CENTURY FOX FILM CORPORATION. ALL RIGHTS RESERVED.

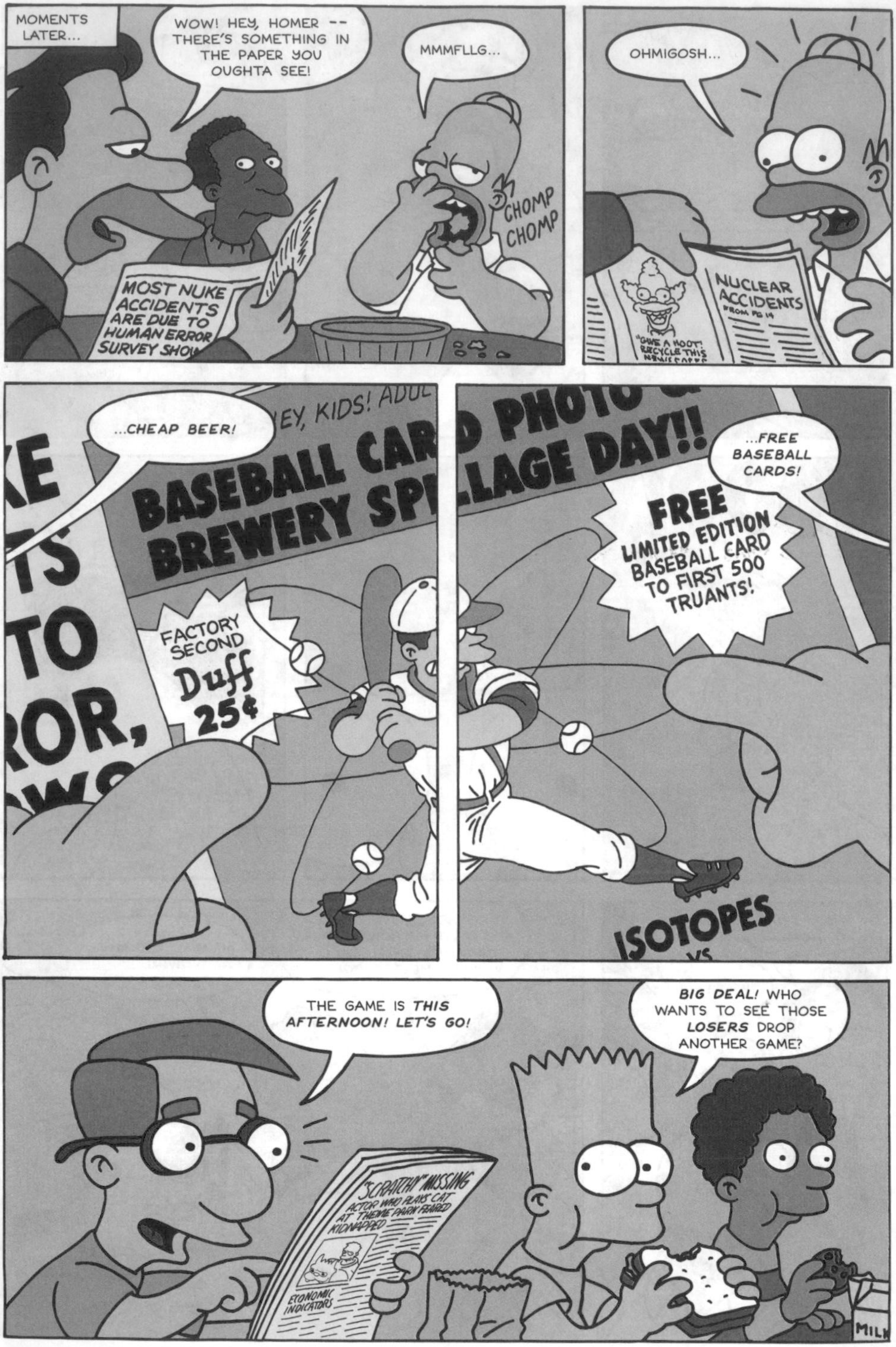
MOMENTS LATER...
WOW! HEY, HOMER -- THERE'S SOMETHING IN THE PAPER YOU OUGHTA SEE!
MMMFLLG...
MOST NUKE ACCIDENTS ARE DUE TO HUMAN ERROR SURVEY SHOW
CHOMP CHOMP
OHMIGOSH...
NUCLEAR ACCIDENTS FROM PG 14
...CHEAP BEER!
BASEBALL CAR D PHOTO & BREWERY SP LLAGE DAY!!
...FREE BASEBALL CARDS!
FREE LIMITED EDITION BASEBALL CARD TO FIRST 500 TRUANTS!
FACTORY SECOND Duff 25¢
ISOTOPES VS
THE GAME IS THIS AFTERNOON! LET'S GO!
BIG DEAL! WHO WANTS TO SEE THOSE LOSERS DROP ANOTHER GAME?
"SCRATCHY" MISSING
ECONOMIC INDICATORS
MILK

103

104

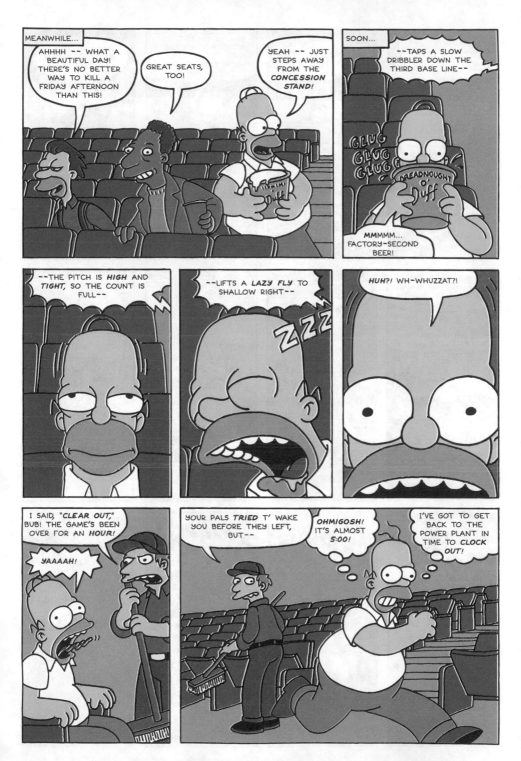

...AND SO, IN CONCLUSION, THIS ISSUE IS YET ANOTHER HIGH-WATER MARK FOR THE ART OF *GRAPHIC STORYTELLING*, DEALING WITH THE ETERNAL THEMES OF GOOD VS. EVIL, UNREQUITED LOVE, AND THE DIFFICULTY OF FINDING A GOOD HAT THESE DAYS. DON'T MISS THE *NEXT THRILLING ISSUE!*

YAY! CLAP! CLAP! CLAP!

WELL, BART...

UH-OH!

...I'M *IMPRESSED!* COMICS ARE VERY CUTTING-EDGE! MS. KRABAPPEL MUST BE *PRETTY HIP* TO HAVE ASSIGNED THIS AS A BOOK REPORT TOPIC! YOU HAVE SOME REAL INSIGHTS INTO THE *SYMBOLIC ASPECTS* OF THE MEDIUM!

???

MEANWHILE...

WHAT IS IT, MISS SIMPSON?

SKRITCH SKRITCH

SKRITCH SKRITCH

MISS KELP, I CAN'T HELP THINKING THAT, AH... INTERESTING AS IT MAY BE TO EXPLORE THE VIEWS OF SUCH AN...INFLUENTIAL THINKER, IT MIGHT BE MORE WORTHWHILE IF WE EACH WROTE *OUR OWN* THOUGHTS, RATHER THAN *COPYING* SOMETHING OUT OF A BOOK!

THAT WAY WE COULD PRACTICE BOTH OUR PENMANSHIP *AND* OUR COMPOSITION SKILLS AT THE SAME --

MISS KELP

WHAT?! ARE YOU CRITICIZING THE BOOK I ASSIGNED YOU?

CAPITALISM AND FREEDOM MILTON FRIEDMAN

I'M MERELY SUGGESTING A WAY TO *ENRICH THE LEARNING EXPERIENCE* FOR ALL OF US. ISN'T THAT WHAT SCHOOL IS FOR?

I HAD YOU PEGGED AS A *TROUBLEMAKER!* THE PURPOSE OF SCHOOL IS TO TEACH YOU *OBEDIENCE, DISCIPLINE,* AND *RESPECT FOR AUTHORITY!*

BUT WE'RE *CHILDREN!* EACH OF US HAS AN INNATE *INDIVIDUALITY* THAT YEARNS TO BE *RESPECTED* AND *NURTURED!*

SUPPRESS IT.

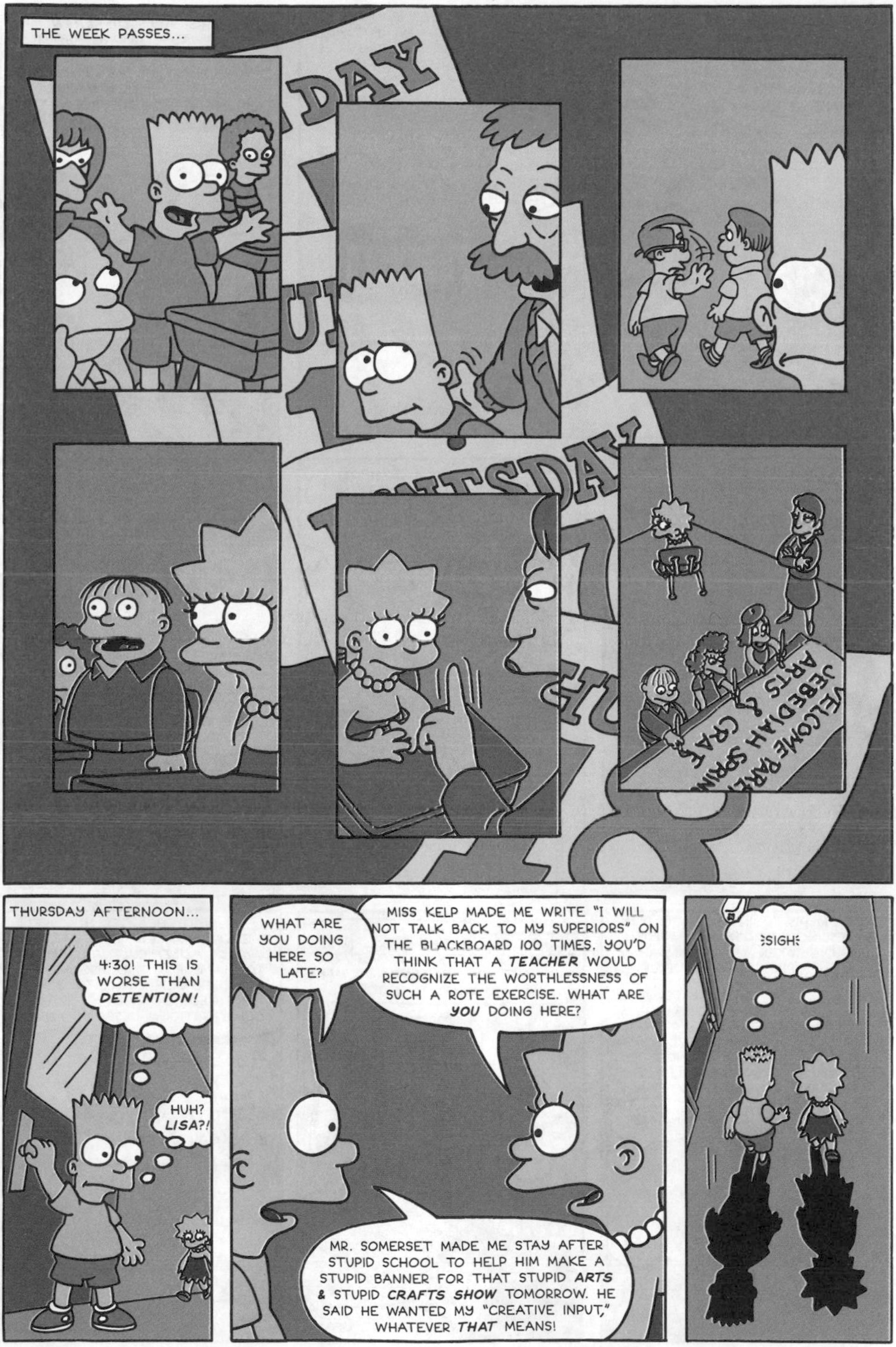

THE WEEK PASSES...
THURSDAY AFTERNOON...
4:30! THIS IS WORSE THAN *DETENTION*!
HUH? *LISA?!*
WHAT ARE YOU DOING HERE SO LATE?
MISS KELP MADE ME WRITE "I WILL NOT TALK BACK TO MY SUPERIORS" ON THE BLACKBOARD 100 TIMES. YOU'D THINK THAT A *TEACHER* WOULD RECOGNIZE THE WORTHLESSNESS OF SUCH A ROTE EXERCISE. WHAT ARE *YOU* DOING HERE?
MR. SOMERSET MADE ME STAY AFTER STUPID SCHOOL TO HELP HIM MAKE A STUPID BANNER FOR THAT STUPID *ARTS* & STUPID *CRAFTS SHOW* TOMORROW. HE SAID HE WANTED MY "CREATIVE INPUT," WHATEVER *THAT* MEANS!
:SIGH:

THE NEXT MORNING...

BYE, KIDS! SEE YOU AFTER SCHOOL AT YOUR ARTS & CRAFTS SHOW!

WHAT AM I GONNA DO? MS. KRABAPPEL NEVER WOULD'VE EXPECTED ANYTHING FROM ME, BUT MR. SOMERSET ASSUMES I'VE DONE SOME BIG DEAL PIECE OF ART FOR THIS SHOW -- AND I DIDN'T DO *ANYTHING*! HE'S GONNA *FLUNK ME* FOR SURE!

HEE HEE! SORRY, BART, BUT I CAN'T HELP LAUGHING AT THE IRONY OF THE SITUATION! AFTER ALL, *YOU'RE* THE ONE WHO SAID THAT IF A TEACHER LIKES YOU, YOU CAN GET AWAY WITH *ANYTHING*!

BUT THIS GUY'S *DIFFERENT*! HE'S ALWAYS TALKING ABOUT *SYMBOLS* AND STUFF. I DON'T KNOW WHAT HE MEANS HALF THE TIME -- HEY, MAYBE THAT'S IT! LET'S SEE...

HERE, BOY!

?

HEY, TEACHER'S PET, WHAT'S WITH THE STICK?

IT'S NOT A STICK, MAN, IT'S...

...IT'S A *SYMBOL*! IT REPRESENTS THE FRAGILE STATE OF OUR NATURAL ENVIRONMENT...

ME PA SH SPRI CRAFTS

???

I DON'T GET IT, MARGE -- IT STILL LOOKS LIKE A STICK.

...OR MAYBE IT REPRESENTS THE, UH, TRAGIC LONELINESS OF THE HUMAN CONDITION, OR...

BART, I'M DISAPPOINTED. INSTEAD OF EXPRESSING YOUR OWN CREATIVITY, YOU'VE TAKEN THE EASY WAY OUT--COPYING SOMEONE ELSE!

THIS PIECE IS SO OBVIOUSLY DERIVATIVE OF THE WORK OF DADAIST MASTER *MARCEL DUCHAMP*! I'M GOING TO GIVE YOU AN "F" AS A REMINDER TO REALLY *CHALLENGE YOURSELF* NEXT TIME.

≩MOAN≩

MEANWHILE...

THIS SAND CASTING REPRESENTS THE *MANY RACES AND CULTURES* WHO HAVE *JOINED HANDS* TO MAKE OUR CITY WHAT IT IS TODAY.

WHISK!

EXCELLENT, LISA--

-- I WHOLEHEARTEDLY AGREE! THE *EVIL FORCES* OF POLITICALLY CORRECT *MULTI-CULTURALISM* ARE TO BLAME FOR THE DISGRACEFUL CONDITION OF OUR CITY! YOUR FINE PIECE OF RIGHT-THINKING SOCIAL CRITICISM DESERVES AN "A"!

BUT *THAT'S* NOT WHAT I *MEANT* --

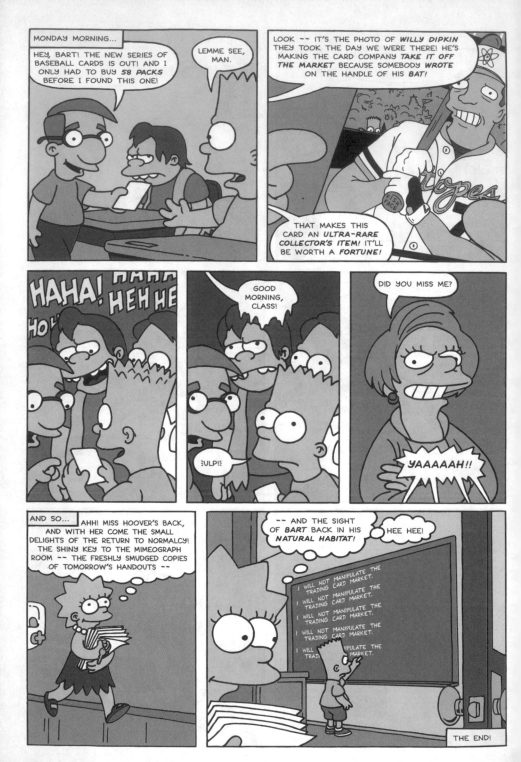

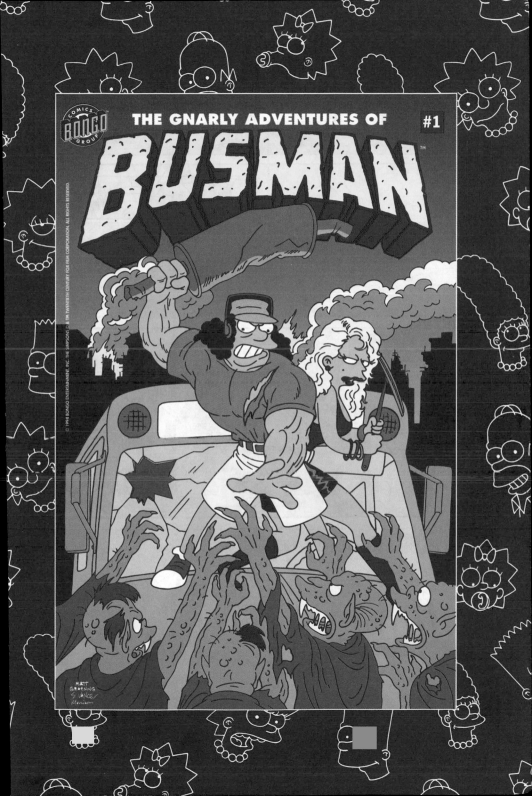

THE DESERT. A ROAD STRETCHES ACROSS THIS BARREN WASTELAND, FLAT AND STRAIGHT LIKE THE NECK OF A REALLY, REALLY HUGE GUITAR, ONLY IT'S MADE OF CONCRETE AND HAS A YELLOW LINE DOWN THE MIDDLE OF IT.

FEW DARE TRAVEL HERE, FOR, IN THE YEARS SINCE THE *NUCLEAR WAR*, THIS HAS BECOME THE DOMAIN OF THE *MUTANT VAMPIRES*, THESE REALLY GNARLY DUDES WITH GREAT BIG POINTY TEETH.

IT IS A *HARD* WORLD -- A *LONELY* WORLD -- A *DANGEROUS* WORLD.

NOWHERESVILLE

ALL KINDS OF *SCARY STUFF* LURKS AROUND EVERY CORNER.

SPLAT

BUT THIS IS *MY* WORLD.

I AM...

BUSMAN

STEVE VANCE
SCRIPT, LAYOUTS

BILL MORRISON
PENCILS

TIM BAVINGTON
INKS

CINDY VANCE
COLORS

MATT GROENING
FELLOW TRAVELLER

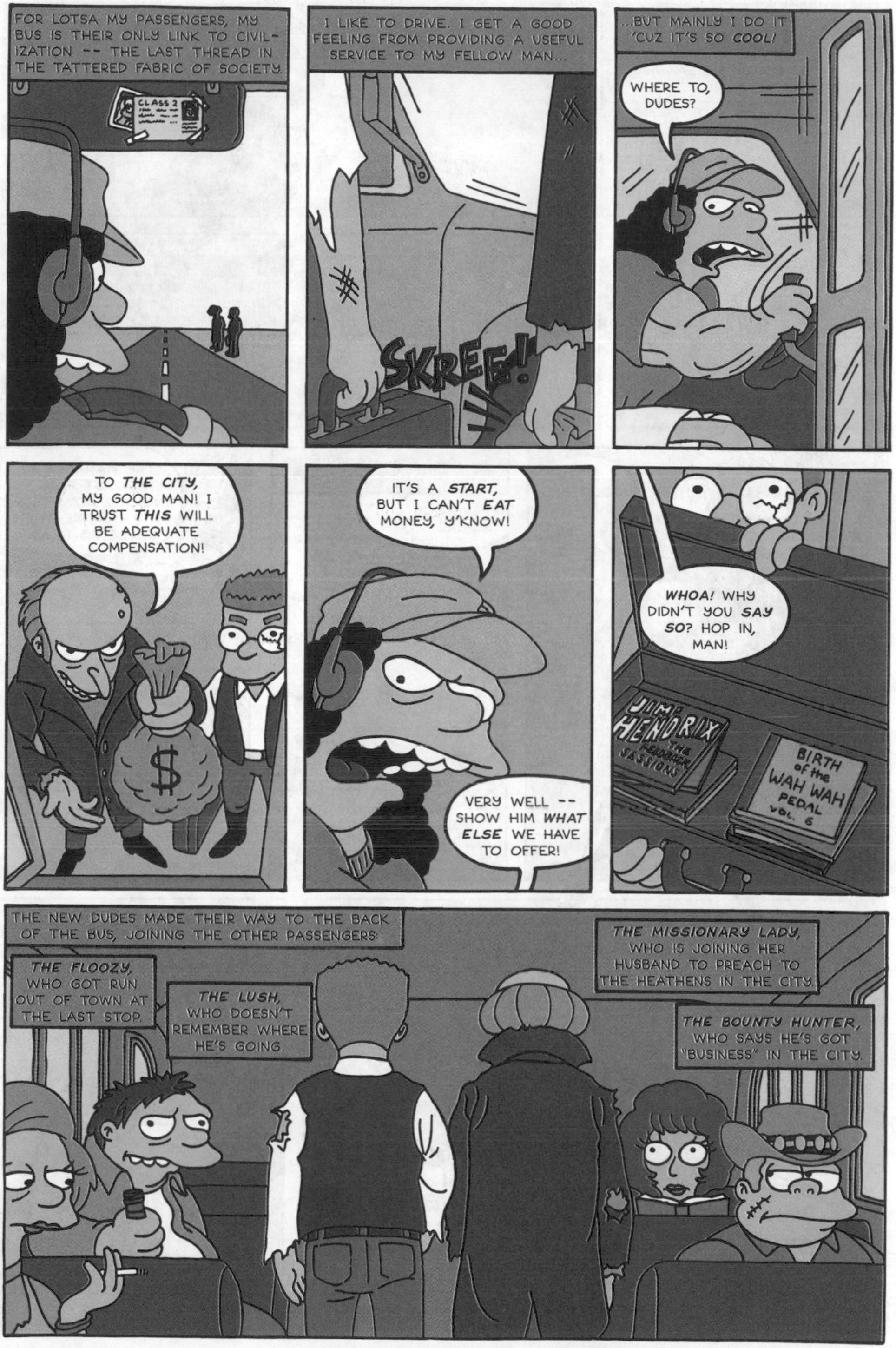
FOR LOTSA MY PASSENGERS, MY BUS IS THEIR ONLY LINK TO CIVILIZATION -- THE LAST THREAD IN THE TATTERED FABRIC OF SOCIETY.
CLASS 2
I LIKE TO DRIVE. I GET A GOOD FEELING FROM PROVIDING A USEFUL SERVICE TO MY FELLOW MAN...
SKREE!
...BUT MAINLY I DO IT 'CUZ IT'S SO COOL!
WHERE TO, DUDES?
TO THE CITY, MY GOOD MAN! I TRUST THIS WILL BE ADEQUATE COMPENSATION!
$
IT'S A START, BUT I CAN'T EAT MONEY, Y'KNOW!
VERY WELL -- SHOW HIM WHAT ELSE WE HAVE TO OFFER!
WHOA! WHY DIDN'T YOU SAY SO? HOP IN, MAN!
JIMI HENDRIX THE FEEDBACK SESSIONS
BIRTH of the WAH WAH PEDAL VOL. 6
THE NEW DUDES MADE THEIR WAY TO THE BACK OF THE BUS, JOINING THE OTHER PASSENGERS:
THE FLOOZY, WHO GOT RUN OUT OF TOWN AT THE LAST STOP.
THE LUSH, WHO DOESN'T REMEMBER WHERE HE'S GOING.
THE MISSIONARY LADY, WHO IS JOINING HER HUSBAND TO PREACH TO THE HEATHENS IN THE CITY.
THE BOUNTY HUNTER, WHO SAYS HE'S GOT "BUSINESS" IN THE CITY.